RELATIONSHIPS MAKE THE DIFFERENCE

Connect with your students and help them build social, emotional, and academic skills

PAT TROTTIER

Pembroke Publishers Limited

Dedication

*To my caring, talented student teachers and future teachers following in your footsteps.
Love your students and champion their causes.
Continue to make a difference by believing you can.*

© 2016 Pembroke Publishers
538 Hood Road
Markham, Ontario, Canada L3R 3K9
www.pembrokepublishers.com

Distributed in the U.S. by Stenhouse Publishers
480 Congress Street
Portland, ME 04101
www.stenhouse.com

All rights reserved.
No part of this publication may be reproduced in any form or by any means electronic or mechanical, including photocopy, scanning, recording, or any information, storage or retrieval system, without permission in writing from the publisher. Excerpts from this publication may be reproduced under licence from Access Copyright, or with the express written permission of Pembroke Publishers Limited, or as permitted by law.

Every effort has been made to contact copyright holders for permission to reproduce borrowed material. The publishers apologize for any such omissions and will be pleased to rectify them in subsequent reprints of the book.

Library and Archives Canada Cataloguing in Publication

Trottier, Patricia Ann, author
    Relationships make the difference : connect with your students and help them build social, emotional and academic skills / Pat Trottier.

Issued in print and electronic formats.
ISBN 978-1-55138-314-9 (paperback).--ISBN 978-1-55138-917-2 (pdf)

    1. Teacher-student relationships. 2. Parent-teacher relationships. I. Title.

LB1033.T763 2016   371.102'3   C2016-903252-3
                                         C2016-903253-1

Editor: Kat Mototsune
Cover Design: John Zehethofer
Typesetting: Jay Tee Graphics Ltd.

Printed and bound in Canada
9 8 7 6 5 4 3 2 1

Contents

Introduction 5

Acknowledgments 7

Chapter 1: The Other *R* in Education 9

Your Relationships with Students 9
Relationships in the Classroom 10
Involving Parents 11
Building the Teaching Community 12
Working Together 12

Chapter 2: Building a Relationship with Your Students 13

Welcome to Our Classroom 14
    Class Rules 15
    Routines 17
Getting to Know Your Students 19
Opening Doors for Students 21
    Developing Boundaries 22
    Nurturing and Improving Self-Confidence 23
    Nurturing and Improving Self-Regulation 24
    Establishing Enduring Relationships 25

Chapter 3: The Classroom Community 33

Moral Intelligences 34
    Kindness 35
    Respect 36
    Empathy 37
    Fairness 38
    Self-Control 39
    Tolerance 40
    Conscience 41

Chapter 4: The Responsive Classroom 57

Sample Strategies for the Responsive Classroom 57
    The Language of Community 57
    Social Stories 58
    The Morning Meeting 59
    Community Involvement 60

    Class Outings *61*
Cross-Curricular Learning *62*
    Sample Lessons *63*

Chapter 5: Taking Relationships Home *65*

Daily Conversations *67*
Organizing Classroom Orientations *69*
Home Visits and Phone Calls *70*
Setting Goals Together *71*
Class and School Websites *73*
Parent Volunteers *73*

Chapter 6: The Teaching Community *77*

The School Team *77*
    School Administration *77*
    Teaching Colleagues *78*
    Student Services/Resource/Guidance *79*
    Classroom Support *80*
The Community Team *81*
    Social Workers *82*
    Psychologists *82*
    Speech and Language Clinicians *83*
    Therapists *84*

Chapter 7: Working Together as a Learning Community *85*

    An Aboriginal Perspective *85*

Resources *91*

Index *93*

Introduction

> It was Spirit Week at school and everyone had their hair done up for Wacky Hair day. Students were placed in working groups for a science lesson to learn more about plants and how they helped our communities. I stopped at one group to start a conversation with a student; he wasn't participating in the group work and was sitting back and uninvolved. I looked at this student and he looked back at me. I couldn't tell if he was just uninterested or if he expected me to scold him for not being involved with his group. His eyes were glazed over and his affect was flat—but not his hair, which was spiked up. I immediately thought of a way to engage him in a conversation: "I really like your hair. How did you get it so high?" His face opened up, and he smiled and proceeded to tell me how he had done his hair all by himself that morning. Then another boy in the group asked him what kind of gel he had used. A three-way conversation about making our hair stand up tall ensued. When the other student moved away to work on his group project, I asked the first student his name. As I tried to pronounce it, he corrected me; I repeated his name again correctly. This student and I had connected; the student appeared relaxed and was sitting forward in his chair. When I asked the student what he could do to help his group, he decided to draw a sun for the group poster. As the class continued, this student who looked like he hadn't wanted to talk to me before was all smiles and had lots to share with me each time I dropped in on his group.

I am writing this book to detail the dynamics of relationships; to show how a teacher can maneuver around the hurdles and road blocks that some students try to put in our way to stop this connection. With a lot of observation and figuring out what tactics work best with which students, teachers can build relationships with all of their students, those who always want to connect and equally those who like to stay off the radar and not be noticed.

    I found out early in my teaching career that I could do a more thorough job in helping students achieve their best when I took the time to get to know my students and their families; students would become part of their own team. When students knew that I cared and was listening and trying to understand what was important to them, they would put extra effort into their work. My caring motivated my students to do their best and, even when they couldn't, they would try harder next time; they found positive benefits through trying. Parents would see their child's efforts and would have more meaningful conversations about their dreams and goals for their children; the parent and child were feeling connected with the school. Through this a trusting relationship was built among the child, parent, and myself.

This connection with my students and their families has taught me a lot about walking in another person's shoes and trying to understand what it's like to live their life, remembering to tolerate differences by showing respect, using self-control even when I am upset, being fair to all my students and their families, doing the right thing, and showing kindness first. I have never met a child I haven't loved and a parent I can't be friends with. It's our job as teachers to find out what works best for each child and family. Each child's social and emotional learning goes hand-in-hand with his/her academic learning, and the classroom sets the scene for growth in each area. If we don't provide this opportunity for children to develop their social and emotional skills, we are missing the best opportunity to ensure children will grow up to be happy, grounded, knowledgeable adults. We must build the supports around students so they can learn to effectively communicate and work with their peers.

> As a school we were taking time to highlight different challenges for children, such as anxiety and depression. It was part of our schoolwide goal of working at being tolerant. We had personnel from the Anxiety Clinic come in and involve three classrooms in a sharing circle. Students were given information about anxiety and depression, and then were encouraged to discuss and ask questions of the presenters. All of our students were mature in their listening and later in asking questions. They were confident in sharing their personal experiences that showed how people in their families suffered from the same or similar problems. When children were respected and given the opportunity to understand, they demonstrated that they took the discussion and sharing seriously through their valuable contributions.

My intent for this book is to take you into my classroom and show you how I work with students and their families, and how I access the daily supports of administration, staff, division, and community agency supports. Effort is put into modeling and designing opportunities for students to learn how to work together with classmates and adults in their lives, as their social and emotional learning is always connected to their academic learning. I have worked in five school divisions, and each division has provided a wealth of ideas, support, and energy to my students, their families, and myself. It's always exciting, pleasantly challenging, and forever rewarding. This book welcomes you to my world of connecting with students and their families and marks the beginning of our socio-emotional and academic journey together.

Acknowledgments

I would like to thank my 4th- and 5th-year education students, especially Mikayla Harrison, Megan Verrier, Kendra Neustaedter, and Alexis Zimak, who have shared their bright lesson plans, technological wonders, and amazing ideas with me.

Special thanks to the cooperating teachers and school staff for welcoming me into their learning communities and generously sharing their strategies, ideas, lessons, and precious time.

Thank you to all my teaching colleagues, staff, administrators, specialists, students, and parents for showing me the best way to collaborate with them. Special thanks go out to Gerry Noonan, Teresa Shume, Brenda McConaghy, and Ernie Shume.

A big thank you to my supportive family and friends who feel I have an important gift to share.

1

The Other *R* in Education

I enjoy the beginning of each school year because I get to know a whole classroom of new students and their families. It's my job to know what my students are capable of, what's important to their families, and how to get my students working with each other. It's a journey we take together, always having lots of fun and accomplishing tons of learning. At the end of each year it's hard to say goodbye because my students are a respectful, hard-working team with parents who continually listen, support, and share their time and talents with our class.

> A new student had moved into class; in his first week, during circle time, he would constantly pull equipment out and give the teacher a defiant smile when he was reminded to leave the materials in the cupboard. By the next week, his teacher had him sitting on a chair in the back row of the circle, away from the cupboard. He was able to sit for five minutes and not touch any objects or students around him. When he looked like he needed a break, his teacher would take him down the hall for a movement break, and then they would return to class again to finish the lesson. After circle time, a lot of one-on-one time was given to the student to develop his interests in the different learning centres and to help him feel a part of the class. This teacher had a positive but firm approach that supported her students in their learning. In return, students loved being in her classroom.

In building community, children are active participants in learning how to connect with their peers and teachers in meaningful, real-life situations and further developing their academic skills. The teacher models roles for each student to play and, when they run into road blocks such as disagreements with their peers, they are given active support to figure out how to correct and improve their relationship difficulties; students can learn how to help other students resolve conflicts too.

This book contains the scaffolding you will require to support your students in further developing the social, emotional, and academic skills essential to standing tall, being proud of ourselves, and positively connecting and including others in our lives. You will have a positive hand in creating our citizens of tomorrow with your students today.

Your Relationships with Students

Connecting with students starts from the moment you meet them and continues every day afterward, as positive relationships are built one day at a time. A colleague of mine considers acts of kindness, respect, and helpfulness as relationship currency that she and her students daily deposit into their relationship banks. She explains this process by telling the story of the Seven Trees. One of her high-school community initiative committees had a fundraiser and was able to purchase seven trees to beautify the front of the school. The trees were arriving that day at noon and my colleague needed seven strong people to dig the seven holes for the trees before they arrived at school. She had a great relationship with the hockey team; when she approached them and asked them if they could dig the holes for the trees, the students happily agreed. By noon that day there were seven large holes in front of the school waiting for the trees. Many years later she bumped into a former student, one of the boys who had helped dig the holes for the trees. He had since become a law enforcer and every time he passed his former high school he was reminded of the story behind those seven beautiful trees. He remembers the day his teacher asked his group to dig the holes for the trees; he has always been happy that he agreed. My friend had deposited enough into each of these students' banks that they were willing to help her out. You need to always be filling your students' relationship banks to develop a reciprocal relationship where there is give and take.

In order to connect you need to make a daily effort to talk with your students, listen to what's important to them, and be available to help when asked. And it's important that your students can count on you when your help is needed. That's the magic ingredient to building that relationship bank with your students—be available to help when they ask for your help or when you think they need your help. Always make time to talk about what kind of supports you are giving your students so they know that, even if they sometimes don't agree, they will respect your decision because you made the decision out of caring for them.

> Developing our students' social and emotional skills goes hand-in-hand with developing their academic skills; you can't do one without the other. Students develop their skills to a higher level if all three areas are included in their learning.

Relationships in the Classroom

Through building community, children are active participants in learning how to connect with their peers and teachers in meaningful, real-life situations. If you model respect, fairness, kindness, empathy, and tolerance, students can practice and appreciate these behaviors at school. As students run into road blocks, such as disagreements with their peers, you can give them active support to figure out how to correct and improve their relationship challenges.

Students can also learn how to help other students resolve conflicts; as they become confident with their new skills, they will independently help their classmates. By the end of each school year, every child has moved a few steps forward in understanding and demonstrating their skills in positively interacting with their peers and adults. Students will further appreciate their strengths, talents, and challenges because they feel cared for and safe in their school environment.

> An autistic student was included in a class play describing how to care for plants; the play script was built around a small phrase that the child was comfortable in repeating. In another situation his educational assistant sat across from him in the circle and wrote key words on a whiteboard to remind this student how to sit and be focused; he was able to listen to the lesson for five minutes before he needed a movement break. Everyone was happy for his success because the students and adults were part of his classroom plan; students welcomed the opportunity to work with their peer.

It is helpful to get your students involved in sharing during class lessons. When a student teacher and her class were researching what schooling was like during pioneer days, students prepared their own interview list to find out what it was like for their parents when they went to school. I managed to be present when a student talked about her parent's experience going to school in Bangladesh. Her story opened our eyes to all the supports we presently have in our schools. We have running water and toilets; many of our school resources are available to use in our classroom free of charge; we either bus to school or don't have far to walk; our school will provide us a lunch if we can't afford to bring or buy one.

It's important to celebrate as a community as often as we can because everyone likes to have a party, assembly, or get-together to enjoy each other's company. All our celebrations are the result of our daily learning together in pairs, groups, and individually in the classroom or other learning environments. I was invited to attend a Kindergarten celebration lunch just before the holiday break. Students had prepared table decorations and name tags for each person. The teacher had made special cookies with her students with the support of educational assistants and parent volunteers. Parent volunteers spent the morning warming up the turkey, potatoes, gravy, and vegetables. The Kindergarten students invited their Grade 3 Buddies to enjoy lunch with them. Everyone had a special time eating the delicious treats and hearing what the students were planning for their holidays.

The moral intelligences of kindness, respect, empathy, fairness, self-control, tolerance, and conscience are emphasized in a responsive classroom. Research points to a strong link between academic success and social-emotional skills; these skills are stronger and longer lasting if combined together in a lesson, as it provides more connections for students to attach their ideas to.

Involving Parents

It is important to welcome students' parents to their children's learning. In order to develop authentic relationships with students, always take time to nurture friendships with their parents. It's a three-way dynamic, in which the needs of the parent and child are joined with the teacher and the school community. When I connect with a student and his/her family, I get a clearer picture and deeper understanding of the child's talents and needs. I welcome the parents to a team that supports their child. Parents understand their children the best and have useful information to share with his/her teacher.

Conversations before and after class are helpful relationship-builders when dealing with parents and guardians. I found it heartwarming how a grandmother wanted to make a difference in her grandson's life. She didn't want him to deal with the issues her children had had as students and presently have as adults. This grandmother had an important job counselling others in her community; she was happy, confident, and grounded. She would be able to provide a stable environment for her grandson and was making sure he was receiving one. It was helpful to know her life story and what her goals were for her grandson.

I have worked with many wonderful parents and guardians over the years who have greatly enhanced their child's and the class's development. Parents love being active participants in their children's learning and always have special talents to share with the class. As the classroom teacher, you will decide how each parent can support classroom learning so your class runs smoothly and effectively. You can help each parent better understand their child's strengths and areas where they need extra help. Describe for them in detail what support networks are necessary for their child, and welcome these supports/personnel to the child's team; you will help the parent feel comfortable with all the members of the child's support team so everyone can work successfully together.

> One of my students was constantly missing a lot of school. In conversations with her mother and through home visits, I found out that her daughter suffered from severe anxiety and would find every excuse to not go to school. Once I had developed a comfortable relationship with the student and her mom, they became open to meeting a local doctor who specialized in working with students with anxiety. They went for a few meetings and, with this support, the student started to attend school regularly every day.

Building the Teaching Community

As you work hard to develop your classroom team of students and parents, it is important that you include school administration, student services, educational assistants, and teaching colleagues as the core of your School Team. Each person plays a special role in supporting your student learning; remember to bring them onto your student, parent, and teacher team.

Clear, purposeful classroom management techniques are the key to ensuring that all your students are following your lead in and out of the classroom as you are directing their daily learning. It's important to arrange meetings with parents and administration to put together plans for students when they are in need of supports, and then to meet again to review the child's progress and whether changes are needed to the plan. It's important to listen to parents when they are sharing information about their child. We have to make sure we fulfill the promises made at our team meetings and, if we can't, we need to take time to discuss the situation. This sharing and discussing builds trust between the teacher, parent, and child.

My Community Team consists of curriculum coordinators, behavior and hearing specialists, and the school support team of social worker, psychologist, occupational therapist, physiotherapist, and speech and language clinician. These people take our student programs to a higher level where we know through assessments and observations exactly where our students shine and where they need extra help.

Taking the time to share your classroom rules and how you plan to engage your students and their families into learning will likely win your administrator's support. Having excellent classroom management techniques makes your administrator's job easier.

Working Together

When you take the time to work closely with your students and their families, and work collaboratively with your colleagues, staff, and divisional and outside agency supports, you will find that you end up with a lot of exciting projects in your classroom and in your school as a whole. When you have a purpose for learning and work as a community to fulfill this purpose, you end up constantly being involved in planning committees for improving student learning, getting to know and celebrating your school diversity, and finding the many ways that children can show their understanding the best.

See Chapter 7 for an extended example of School and Community Teams working together, documenting an initiative on including Aboriginal perspective in daily curriculum teaching.

2

Building a Relationship with Your Students

From the moment your students arrive in the fall, be waiting for them by their cloakroom/locker area and walk with them back to the classroom. Your actions show students that you care about them being successful learners and focusing on expectations for behavior and attitude. You want them to be happy, be able to connect with yourself and their peers, and put effort into their learning. You like your students and enjoy being with them. Whether they are gifted, average, or challenged, you are the first person in line to ensure students get appropriate academic programs that help them flourish and grow.

It is important to be present when your students first arrive in the morning because it gives you a chance to observe their entrance to the school, their connections with other students, their mood, and if it looks like it will be a good day. If you see any red flags you can start a conversation with a particular student to see if he/she will share more with you. Could the student be hungry because she missed her breakfast and now hunger pains are reminding her she got up late? Is the student rushing through the door because he has something special to show you? Now is the time to learn more about how prepared your students are for school today.

Every day, welcome your students with a smile and say, "Good morning." Then move your students into morning routines; use reminders and encouragement as you listen to their thoughts and questions as you observe their movements and behaviors. At the beginning of each school year and throughout the year, routines can help you do the following:

- Get your classroom space student-ready so it supports connections between the students and yourself. Make sure the environment is hands-on and appealing to students so they are eager to learn.
- On the first day of school, lay out your management strategies and rules, showing students the boundaries for their interactions with each other and with you. These are clear guidelines to follow so students can safely learn to positively connect with each other and the adults in their lives. Develop classroom rules to support the development of academic, social, and emotional skills.
- Design routines and activities to give students the opportunity to practice how to become independent learners, and how to work positively with their peers and adults to complete their work. Hold morning meetings so you and your students get to know each other and have time to discuss, plan, and assess together.
- Take time to consciously observe your students in the first month of school and step in to offer suggestions as to how they can collaborate effectively with their peers. Note which students are not trying to interact and build up opportunities for them to be in groups with nurturing, helpful students who make them feel comfortable. By the time you enter the second month

of school, students should be coming together and understanding what their role is in building the class community.
- Open many doors of opportunity for your students. Your caring for your students nurtures and further develops their self-confidence. When you empower your students with information and skills around building friendships with their peers and the adults in their lives, they start to successfully connect with others on their own without constant direction from the teacher; thus enduring student relationships are developed.

Welcome to Our Classroom

In August, before the school year starts, I send out letters to my new students, welcoming them to my class and reminding them of the date and time of their first school class meeting. I set up learning centres and hold an open house. On that first day, I enjoy watching my students walk through the door with their families. Some bring their whole families, including their siblings; in some cases grandparents come; other students bring one parent. It's rewarding to watch students' eyes dart around the room and to observe which centres they head to first. If they are really excited, they start tugging their parent's arm or just run ahead. Once in their chosen centres, students pick up everything and look through it carefully. If it's a building centre, they will start to model their own structure from a display; in the art centre they will immediately paint a picture or trace a design; in the science centre they will read about an experiment; they will check out the tapes and books in the library. It's very heartwarming to see the child stay in the centres and try to solve a problem together with a family member. I'm drawn into the centres when they have questions or ideas they want to talk about.

In preparation for the first day of school, organize your classroom to be a magnet that will draw in your students and activate their personal curiosity for learning. Students are instantly motivated to explore as they first walk through the classroom door. You don't have to encourage children to get involved with their environment if it's set up to pique their curiosity and activate their need to check out everything. Social, emotional, and academic learning will be lots of fun. Tips for welcoming students:
- Have names ready to label student lockers/cupboards.
- Dust and reorganize cupboards so the first-term materials are at the front.
- Organize centres and have the first centres ready to go.
- Write a welcoming message on the board or interactive whiteboard.
- Prepare a handout that outlines the class program, homework, phone calls, and first-month schedule for parents.

> In the handout, I supply parents with my e-mail address and home phone number for when they have questions.

The focus is on getting to know students for the first month of school; therefore, from the start, set up a hands-on classroom that supports children's learning through their visual, auditory, and kinaesthetic strengths. It's important for your classroom program to include opportunities for students who need to move as they learn; lack of this will cause students to act out in frustration and turn learning into a negative experience. For students who are visual, you will need lots of pictures and visual displays; for auditory students, you will need to provide a lot of specific, detailed instructions, listening centres, and opportunities for discussion. When you include these modalities in each lesson, the needs of all your students will be met.

Students need choices in how they show their learning. I keep this in mind when students are given assignments; they can make choices from different media to show what they have learned. This set-up works for students from Kindergarten to Grade 8, as you display age-appropriate, hands-on curriculum materials for students with supportive directions and modeling.

Consider including the following in your classroom set-up:

- a carpeted meeting area with sitting space for all students (space for chairs too)
- interactive whiteboard/computer in meeting area for reviewing and teaching skills
- your desk/centre, lined up with meeting area so you can use the document camera, projector, etc.
- a listening centre with interesting books and tapes and paper/writing tools for responding
- an art/writing centre with different types of paper, writing tools
- a science/social studies centre with building materials, tape, glue, chart paper, writing tools, resource books

Classroom placement of tables or student desks is an important consideration. You want all students to be comfortable, able to hear and see you, and able to read the board while you and/or other students are presenting. It's necessary to move around as you present a lesson so you can keep your students focused and involved in the class discussion. Your presence can help bring students back to the lesson if they are distracted by their peers or daydreaming.

> You can change your student seating as much as you like; it gives students the chance to learn how to work with many different personalities in their class.

Class Rules

On the first day of school I lay out my management strategies and rules so students are shown boundaries for their interactions with each other and with me. Knowing how to interact with everyone in class and to know how to do it positively will deepen their learning experience. All their talents—social, emotional, and academic—will be developed simultaneously. A set of rules helps everyone work toward getting along as they are learning and completing their tasks. For children it gives parameters for their thinking and behavior. Many come from homes where there are boundaries; they need to learn the parameters of a classroom full of students. The class is a microcosm of the bigger world outside, the playground in which children can learn to be caring, giving, and knowledgeable citizens of the future. Children of all ages are sponges; they soak up information and want to do their best. They are natural helpers from birth and, when given guidance and support, they continue to develop these skills.

Classroom rules should start out simple and grow throughout the year, depending on the personality of the group. Some classes are mature and able to take on more responsibilities within and outside of the classroom. Other classes are less skilled or experienced and need a greater degree of structure and a lot of scaffolding to support them in their learning journey. I remember the different classroom personalities I have worked with over the years. On the first day of school, some classes would be ready to get right into the writing, reading, and completing of assignments; students were focused and full of strong academic skills. Other classes would enter the class by bumping into each other and end up in arguments, unable to sit for more than two minutes or keep discussions on topic. We need to see where students' strengths lie and build from there.

Developing classroom rules with students gets them to be part of the daily decision-making, teaches them the steps they need to take to positively connect with their peers and adults, and lets them experience the joy of having positive relationships. This gets students to actively participate in developing their social and emotional skills as they are learning their academic skills. Keep in mind that each classroom and school will have its own set of rules, emerging from the beliefs and practices of that community and specifically designed to keep everyone on the same page when it comes to behavior expectations and classroom rules. Develop your own classroom rules around these expectations.

Time needs to be taken so children can learn what respect looks like, what it sounds like, and how it makes you feel inside. Students can learn this through role-playing, writing, drawing, and conversations with lots of questions and clarifications. They can post their learning on the wall, on their class website, in the school newsletter; they can help write these beliefs on a chart as they are presented and discussed. These beliefs can be incorporated into your daily curriculum lessons as well.

> I post these three rules in our classroom so we can refer to them whenever necessary.

Sample of Classroom Rules

Rule 1: Students need to show respect for themselves and others. This means they need to speak kindly to their peers/staff inside and outside, and treat classroom/student materials with respect. *My language and actions with students and staff needs to model respect.*

Rule 2: Students need to listen while others are speaking. They can respectfully ask questions for clarification after the person is finished, respond with a positive answer, or not say anything. If they have been asked a question and do not know the answer, they can ask the person for further clarification or their teacher for help. *I need to model good listening skills with my students by showing them how I listen when they speak to me.*

Rule 3: When students disagree they need to do it respectfully and learn to accept that they can't always get what they want. They will learn how to compromise. *I need to model how to disagree in a respectful way and show what compromise looks like and sounds like.*

When you put parameters in place for students in the classroom you give them the chance to learn appropriate behavior. This prepares the child for what is important in life and helps them come to be able to handle themselves on their own when you are not there to guide them. You are giving them tools to be successful for when they are independent and on their own.

I was having a discussion with a student about behavior in class. He said that he was trying not to treat another student as he was being treated. He noticed when his peer acted out in class, not a lot happened. There were no consequences. He noticed that the adults talked about it but didn't do anything beyond that. His teachers hadn't set rules for this kind of behavior. The student I was talking to knew there were no consequences but was wise enough to know that he didn't want to act the same way. As teachers, we need to set up parameters for student behavior and consequences for when these rules are not followed; students need us to be fair at all times. We are their moral compass in class.

It's important for students to have to deal with the aftermath of making a poor decision. If a student says something that hurts another student's feelings, it's important for the student to think about how to help the other person feel better again. Students need to be held accountable for their actions when they hurt others; they need to think about how they are going to resolve the problem and make a better decision next time.

In dealing with children when they have offended others through words or actions, it helps to take the time to get the two students together to talk about what happened. When the story is pieced together and each student has agreed on what occurred, a solution can be found. If there is an aggressor, this person is encouraged to come up with solutions that are acceptable to the student who was offended; through discussion both children together may come up with a solution. In real-life situations, we put parameters in place to guide our students to help them develop empathy for other students. This experience is invaluable, as it will help move students forward in making reasonable, sensible decisions that won't offend their peers. It keeps them on the road to becoming more independent and knowing their job is to be respectful, helpful, and kind to their peers and community.

> Two Grade 1 students got into a physical argument at recess. They both had their own behavior challenges but that day one student's behavior was definitely hurtful: that student pulled off the other student's prosthetic arm and threw it into the mud. At first I checked to make sure each student was okay and that the prosthetic arm was clean and fitting properly. Then we spent a lot of time talking about what happened before the incident, why it happened, and what they could do differently next time. We talked about feelings, because I was worried that it could have been traumatic for the student to have her arm thrown into the mud. We worked out a plan of how to play safely at recess and made time to talk about it before each recess. Parents were contacted and brought into the recess plan to provide extra reminders and backup from home. While I found the situation extremely upsetting, the students were less upset and anxious to play together again at the next recess.

Routines

Along with developing class rules, it's important to start each day with routines and activities that give students the opportunity to practice how to become independent learners and to work positively with peers and adults to complete their work. Our class structures help us all to work better together. Predictable routines further support students in staying focused by grounding them in class and creating a nurturing and safe environment for them to work in.

Daily routines help the classroom hum with positive energy because everyone knows their role. This positive atmosphere takes everyone's learning to deeper levels of understanding and cognition. When students know what to expect and what is expected of them, they are much happier. Routines ensure children are active, purposeful participants in class, connecting positively with peers and adults in their lives.

Routines can be put in place to assist students with managing the following:

- Clothing: Students will be responsible for storing their clothing in an orderly fashion every time they put something in or take something out of their locker.
- Personal work materials: Students will have a plan to keep their work and books neatly stored, whether it is their own desks or shared space. Weekly clean-up periods help students organize their work into manageable pieces; students with weak organizational skills might have to do this on a daily basis. Classroom buddies can help each other to be neat; you can pair students who complement each other's strengths. Time constraints are necessary to keep children focused; e.g., give them ten minutes to do the desk or table organizing.
- Finished work: Have boxes/tables/cupboards set up for students to hand in their finished work. Have another depot where students can pick up marked work. You can have students check work lists to see what they have finished and what needs to be done next. This helps students become more independent in their learning as they see the big learning plan for the unit, term, or season. Children might want to organize their own projects so they can delve further into particular areas of interest. Parent volunteers are very helpful in keeping these stations organized.
- Daily classroom jobs: There are always jobs that need attending to on a regular basis; for example, students can update the date, day of the cycle, and the daily plan (subjects for the day) posted on the board or interactive whiteboard. Following a system in which every student has a classroom job to complete on his/her special day builds knowledge of classroom responsibilities and how to contribute towards the daily running of their class.
- Morning meetings: I like to organize a special class area to meet with my students. It's important that everyone has space to sit on a carpet or in a chair; everyone needs to be comfortable and free from desks. It's our area to sit as a group to talk and share together. I like my students to sit close in front of me so I can look into everyone's eyes as we are sharing. Nobody sits in the back because I need them all to be close; this keeps everyone focused and stops students from daydreaming. Older students prefer to sit in a circle on chairs. It's helpful to have a computer or interactive whiteboard close by so presentations can be made from this spot as well.

Classroom routines teach each child responsibility and a sense of purpose. When students walk into their classroom each day, they know where to start and what to do. Daily routines help students feel comfortable in class and give them opportunities to work positively with their peers. They help children fit in with the classroom dynamics.

When students have trouble with any of these routines, it can guide you in developing supports for students so they can achieve and be successful in completing their daily tasks. Even students with behavior and learning challenges can successfully contribute to their classroom. When you have a united classroom, students and teacher are all responsible to get the learning done. Students learn how to take responsibility for their learning and develop compassion and caring for their peers' and teacher's well-being and learning.

> A Grade 7/8 teacher I worked with found that his students completed their work faster if they had a system for collecting their work and picking up their marked assignments. As a student services teacher, I enjoyed working in his classroom because every student knew what their assignment was (every student had work they were able to complete on their own; some activities were adapted for some students). There was a positive energy in class as every student was focused on his or her assignment. After each lesson, the teacher would pose a question for students to discuss in a group. Students got into their groups and followed previously established discussion guidelines. They had responsibilities to keep their work areas clean and were dismissed at the end of the day only when their areas were tidy. This encouraged students to work together to keep their areas clean and organized.

Getting to Know Your Students

See page 27 for the Parent Invitation to the open house; page 28 for the Parent Survey.

You can start the process of getting to know your students before you even meet them. I send a survey to parents before school starts to get a better idea of each student's strengths and needs. I ask parents to bring the filled-in survey when we meet in the first week of school. At our meeting I encourage parents and children to talk about the survey and I jot down extra notes so I'll remember everything parents have to say about their children. This information helps me decide what lessons to start with and how to plan the lesson so the child will be successful: *Do I need to plan a more challenging activity for this student or does he need the activity to be shorter and easier to tie in with his challenged learning level?*

See pages 29–31 for student form and questionnaires.

My first lessons during the month of September deal with getting to know my students. I have information from their preceding year's teacher and their learning from past years, but I want to know what the child can tell me about him/herself. What are their strengths and abilities? What do they find challenging? I have students individually work on a student questionnaire and have designed forms for their personal learning levels. These are included on pages 29–31; you can adapt them to fit your student needs. When students are overwhelmed by writing, I ask them to start by drawing about themselves. If they need someone to scribe their thoughts on paper, my educational assistant or I will do this for the student.

> In a Grade 5 lesson on Pioneer Homes, a fifth-year student teacher developed a social studies lesson around Early Pioneer Schools. To help students understand the differences and similarities between school then and today, she asked her students to interview their parents about what going to school was like when they were younger. She brainstormed and collaborated with her students to develop the interview questions they used. Her students come from many different countries and continents. It was especially interesting to hear a student read a story about her parents from Bangladesh and how they went to school. It helped everyone in class to understand her family better and walk in their footsteps for a while.

> Grade 5 students studying Pioneers in Social Studies developed a list of questions to use when they interviewed their family about what it was like growing up in their community 20, 30, or 40 years ago. Students could write the answers to the following questions with their family members or choose to make a more detailed presentation with a video, voice recording, poster, etc.
> 1. Where were you born?
> 2. Where did you grow up and what was it like?
> 3. Can you tell me what you remember about my grandparents (your parents)?
> 4. What was your lifestyle like growing up?
> 5. What was your home (apartment, house, farm, etc.) like? How many rooms?
> 6. What did you do in your free time?
> 7. What kind of jobs did you have?
> 8. What do you remember about school?
> 9. Did you have pets?
> 10. What are some interesting stories or memories that stick out in your mind?
> 11. What were some of your chores growing up?
> 12. Do you have any pictures, videos, or books that you could share with me?

There are precious rewards when you take the time to get to know your students. This information will direct you in helping every child be successful in your class. Knowledge points you to the strengths and needs of each child. When you gather this information you can start building a program that will support each child's growth and development.

Take time to observe your students to check how they are doing. I remember being on morning patrols and crossing a student in the morning who was smiling and walking with a bounce to his step. Later that morning I saw him sitting on a step in our front entrance and his face was white and he looked as if he had seen a ghost. I approached him and asked to speak to him privately. He told me he had got a message on his e-mail and it was very upsetting. I remember sharing my observations with his mother; she checked into the e-mail. He may have been dabbling with some questionable Internet sites, so my contact with the parent led her to set more boundaries for her son while he was online. It's important to know our students and let that knowledge spur our actions when we think they need our help.

> A young child in my class started to try to run onto a busy street while we were waiting for the school bus; it was obvious she was trying to hurt herself. She was in foster care and not feeling wanted or loved and she needed someone to listen to her. After many phone calls to our Child and Family agency and her psychologist, another foster family was found for this girl. It was heartwarming one day to see her get into the backseat of her new family's car. Her foster mom was smiling and put her arm around her and hugged her tight. She finally found a family that loved her and wanted her.

When you take time to get to know your students and understand what's important to them, you will be able to help them when they need your assistance. Developing relationships with our students means being continually observant of them, getting involved in their conversations, and finding out what is important to them. Listening to how they say something as well as what they say is important too. I had a Grade 8 student who found out she needed to wear glasses. When she brought her glasses to school, she didn't want to put them on. School staff and her peers continued to encourage her. One day I gathered her with all of her peers who wore glasses and we took a picture of everyone wearing glasses. Students were given copies of the picture and eventually this student started to wear her glasses to school too.

Opening Doors for Students

Your connection with your students gives them the opportunity to be involved in positive, nurturing, and healthy relationships. For students who come from homes without support and boundaries, this relationship lets the child know what caring relationships are all about.

Setting boundaries and expectations at home and school makes life more manageable for teachers, parents, and students. In order for students to be able to make responsible decisions as they get older, they need to have parameters set on their actions and behavior all through their formative years at school. Through the safety of these boundaries, children can practice appropriate social skills and follow a schedule with class rules. They will learn how to deal with failure when they challenge these boundaries and then how to deal with the consequences—perfect training in becoming an independent adult.

When you work on building relationships you start to notice that your students are paying more attention to what you are saying. They are learning that you really care about them and how they succeed in school. They start to try a bit harder and, if they have behavior issues, they will become more open to working towards resolving them. For every child, the nurturing will affect them differently.

My students knew the classroom rules so well that they could describe them to anyone without any prompts from me. They knew exactly why it was important to behave appropriately in class, how to treat their peers, and the quality of work I expected from them. We talked every day, constantly interacting with each other, working towards developing positive relationships, learning new concepts, and demonstrating our knowledge of new learning. Everyone cared for each other because it was important in our learning community. My students' parents would report to me that their child would come home saying, "Mrs. T. said it was important to do it this way." As a teacher I hear these same comments from my friends about their children, and I know their children's teacher has taken the time to connect with students and the children are feeling a part of and supported in their learning community. They have been given the words to talk about what's important in their lives and shown how to positively connect with their teacher and peers as they develop their academic and social skills. Every day my students are getting to know me better as I get to know them better too.

Building positive and caring relationships with our students helps to move them further along in becoming emotionally and socially independent. It nudges them forward to participate in relating with others. When they do this, positive outcomes always happen. When students are encouraged to show positive behavior toward others, they get instantaneous results. They will be greeted with a warm smile or a positive comment: "Aren't you helpful/kind/thoughtful." The positive nature of these exchanges motivates the child to keep coming back for more. Everyone likes the positive strokes that they receive after successful exchanges.

> I worked with a Grade 6 student who did not want to have anything to do with me. I was a resource teacher and he saw me as somebody telling him he couldn't learn and be successful. Even though I tried hard to make our group work interesting, he would start each session by saying he didn't want to come and that he "wasn't dumb." I organized a peer mentoring opportunity for him so he could read to a Grade 2 student and help the younger student feel comfortable reading his own levelled books. My Grade 6 student loved being a helper and, in turn, he became more positive about my working with him to improve his spelling and writing skills. I made sure to connect with his mother to let her know what I was doing and how her son loved reading and helping another student. By knowing my student, I knew how to help build a more positive relationship. His mother became a positive supporter too; together we helped her son build confidence in himself and feel comfortable with getting help. Several years later I met this student with his father in the community and he shared that he was having great success with his welding course in high school. His father was beaming from ear to ear with pride for his son.

When we take time to connect with our students we give students a voice. When I spoke to a handful of Grade 7 and 8 students about what was important to them, they shared the following ideas:
- Morning meetings gave them a way to connect with their teacher and peers in a nonthreatening and relaxed way.
- They wanted their teacher to look after their needs; if you know they are going to fool around, you can help them not to do this.
- They wanted changes to the environment to look after their needs.
- They wanted fair rules in their class. When a student doesn't follow the rules, they wanted the teacher to get involved and make sure the consequences are fair.
- "Some kids learn differently than others. Treat kids according to their needs."

Developing Boundaries

Students need to know what their boundaries are for behavior in the classroom and at school. Establishing boundaries would include asking the following:
- What is acceptable behavior with their peers, teacher, and other adults at school?
- What is their job in class?
- How can they contribute to their class learning?

Some classes demonstrate the behaviors in the sample and don't need reminders to develop these skills. Boundaries set at the beginning of the year can be changed throughout the year as students mature and grow; more can be expected of students as their skills develop.

> *Sample Classroom Behavior Boundaries*
>
> 1. Keep your hands and feet to yourself. When you are sitting in a morning meeting or circle time, don't touch other students. You can keep your hands in your lap or by your side.
> 2. Talk with an inside voice. You can practice what this sounds like.
> 3. When your teachers or peers are talking to you, stop what you are doing, look them in the eye, and listen to what they are saying.
> 4. If you are upset and need help to control yourself, let a friend know or tell the teacher.
> 5. If you demonstrate inappropriate behavior, even after getting help from inside the class, then you need to go to the office and see the principal, go for a movement break, or go to the washroom. The teacher will decide what you need.

In developing boundaries the teacher should work on one behavior at a time, model the behavior, and get other students to model as well. Extra practice helps students understand what the behavior looks and sounds like. The behavior can be written into a story, play, or poster for more practice. You need to model the behavior at all times and, when students forget to demonstrate it, use the experience as a learning moment for everyone.

Nurturing and Improving Self-Confidence

When you let children know you are interested in their welfare, they will become more confident. Your caring shows that they matter. They will consider trying things you suggest because they start to believe in themselves and that they can affect change. They have the power within themselves to be successful.

> One student struggled in Kindergarten and Grade 1 because he couldn't connect with his teacher and peers. He was in a multi-age group and had been with the teacher for two years. His teacher never gave up on him; she took time to tell and show him what behavior he needed to demonstrate and how he could follow through on this. Finally, one day the student and teacher had a reciprocal conversation about what his behavior needed to look like and how to achieve that. His teacher was able to recall behaviors she had observed the day before and tie them into behaviors the child was demonstrating that day. The child was able to see the connection and told his teacher he was going to try to do the same thing that day. This child was beginning to express his understanding about the type of positive behavior he needed to practice. At that moment he started thinking of himself as an individual with the power to make changes in his behavior. He demonstrated a move toward being more independent in making appropriate decisions. This, in turn, increased his interest in completing his assignments.

When students are given information on how to keep themselves safe and feel comfortable sharing with their teacher, they will have the confidence to ask for help. Years ago I was working with students in a Grade 2 classroom and we were talking about personal safety. The students had learned about what to do if somebody was touching them in an inappropriate way. Armed with the knowledge that it was okay to say *no* to negative touching, a child disclosed to me that he was being touched in his home. He had told this person *no*, but the abuse was continuing. I shared this disclosure with my principal, who contacted our Child and Family agency to get protection for the child.

Nurturing and Improving Self-Regulation

Self-regulation is a complex and multi-faceted skill. It is also related to self-confidence. Students will take your suggestions and try them out because they want to be successful in their learning, because you have taught them that they matter and how to be successful.

Knowing what is coming and how to prepare for it emotionally is key to self-regulation. As part of demonstrating respect toward my students, I make a point of letting students know when transitions will occur in class. Some students are able to move from one activity/situation to another; others require warning ahead of time so they can successfully switch their attention. A prompt helps prepare students for the upcoming change. I helps some students wind down from their current involvement and prime their mindset to be ready for the move to the next activity. It can be a helpful reminder for students to speed up what they are doing or work harder at completing their present task. For students who find change difficult, prompting a transition helps them move forward without losing control of their emotions. Some useful tools can help students ready themselves for change:

- using a timer on the student's desk
- learning how to tell time on the classroom clock
- a soothing personal reminder that student and teacher have established beforehand, such as a tap on the shoulder, a smile, or pointing to the clock

Another way to help students learn to self-regulate is to help them build a personal social story about what it looks like and sounds like when they are self-regulated. You can take this story further and have students act out what self-regulating looks and sounds like. Students can think of times when they felt out of control and not regulated, and then brainstorm other ways to handle the situation. The more students involved in thinking about their behavior and how they can change negative behaviors, the more practice they will get in thinking and acting in the moment.

> For more on personal social stories, see page 58.

Students will have better personal self-regulation if they are given the correct academic program to follow. If a student needs more challenges in his/her learning, then time needs to be taken to do this. Usually it helps to collaborate with the student so you can organize a topic that is interesting and motivating. If students are not interested in their learning, they might take other students off track and cause a lack of focus in class. Some students need their program adapted because learning will be successful for students only when they can understand and work at it. If the work is too difficult, the child can get frustrated and possibly lose his/her temper in class or on the playground.

> I once worked with a Grade 8 student who was able to work at a high-school level in math. Using consultation with teachers at the local high school, we were able to get a math program that was challenging and interesting for her. She was not wasting her time completing Grade 8 math that she had mastered years before.

Establishing Enduring Relationships

When you work on connecting with your students, you help them feel safe in class. When they feel safe, they are more likely to take risks and try things they wouldn't have had the confidence to try before. When students start to feel the trust you have in them, they will show what they are able to do and what they are interested in. They will be open to show their strengths and weak areas. From this you will have a better idea of how to plan your lessons so they can experience more success and want to learn more.

By modeling tolerance and respect in a Kindergarten classroom I helped to nurture students in developing their own support system for an autistic classmate. It began when one student said she had a headache because another student, who was autistic, was making too much noise. I explained to her that her classmate had very few words to express himself, and that's why he would make noises; if we were patient the student would learn more language. I suggested she invite him to play with her so she could help him be part of her group and learn more language, and she could be like a big sister to him. Once she understood, the student would patiently welcome her autistic classmate into her play. To support this development I interviewed each child to find out what was important to him/her and we wrote up little books together. Each child made a presentation to the class about themselves. I made a joint presentation with the student with autism and everyone got to find out what was special for him. When the autistic child had difficulty leaving a gym class, another child came up and offered to help him leave. He said he knew what to do: he took his classmate's hand and encouraged him to leave the gym, talking to the other child as they walked out of the gym and back to their classroom. This child had already found a way to connect with his peer and was confident to share his strategy on his own. These experiences helped the autistic student to develop a larger repertoire of language to express himself.

> One time I got to work with the same group of students for three years. After teaching them Kindergarten, I moved to teaching a Grade 1/2 combined class. Having these students over three years meant there was no down time at the beginning of each year, when it usually takes a few months to get to know my students. I knew these students' talents and challenges so well that their learning never skipped a beat. It allowed most of our learning to be cross-curricular. The Grade 2 students decided they wanted to write a play about living in medieval times; the lead writers turned out to be the King and Queen in the story. The students wrote the play and assigned parts to all Grade 1 and 2 students. We practiced daily

When you empower students by scaffolding their learning around building friendships with their peers and the adults in their lives, you make their learning deeper and broader. This will be discussed in more detail in Chapter 4: The Responsive Classroom.

> and, when everyone felt comfortable, we invited individual classrooms to come and watch our play. Parents were invited one day to watch as well. To highlight their writing, students wrote their play out in story form and illustrated each page with colorful pictures. Many years later I met the King from our Grade 1/2 play at a school I was assigned to for a term position—but he wasn't a student there. He had become a talented, hard-working high-school teacher who ran an amazing program for young adults in trouble with the law.

Take the time to listen to your students and let them know you care. You are there for them and they can trust you will help them. Praise your students for their strengths and help them when they meet challenges. They will feel you are their friend and probably remember you as a special teacher. You want to make a difference in every child's life.

Parent Invitation

Date: _____

Dear Parents/Guardians,

I am very happy that _____ will be in my class this year.

You are invited to attend an Open House on _____ , _____ at _____ School.

Your appointment is scheduled for _____. If this time is not convenient, please

phone our office secretary to reschedule. The office number is _____.

Please fill out the attached survey with your child and bring this with you to the Open House. We can talk about your completed survey at our meeting.

Your child will be able to try out our Science and Library Centres during your visit and can take home activities to share with your family.

Here is my school e-mail address if you need to contact me before this date:

_____

I am looking forward to meeting you at our Open House.

Sincerely,

Parent Survey

Date: _____

Dear _____,

Please fill out this questionnaire so I can get to know your child better. You can return it to me at our first meeting on _____ at _____.

Child's birthdate and where he/she was born: _____

At home my child likes to_____.

In the community my child likes to_____.

My child's favorite thing to do is_____.

My child needs help with_____.

☐ I would like to share more with you at a later date

I would like to

☐ Volunteer in class

☐ Prepare materials at home

☐ Go on field trips

☐ Prepare a snack for birthdays

The best phone number to use to contact me: _____

My email address: _____

Student Graphic Organizer

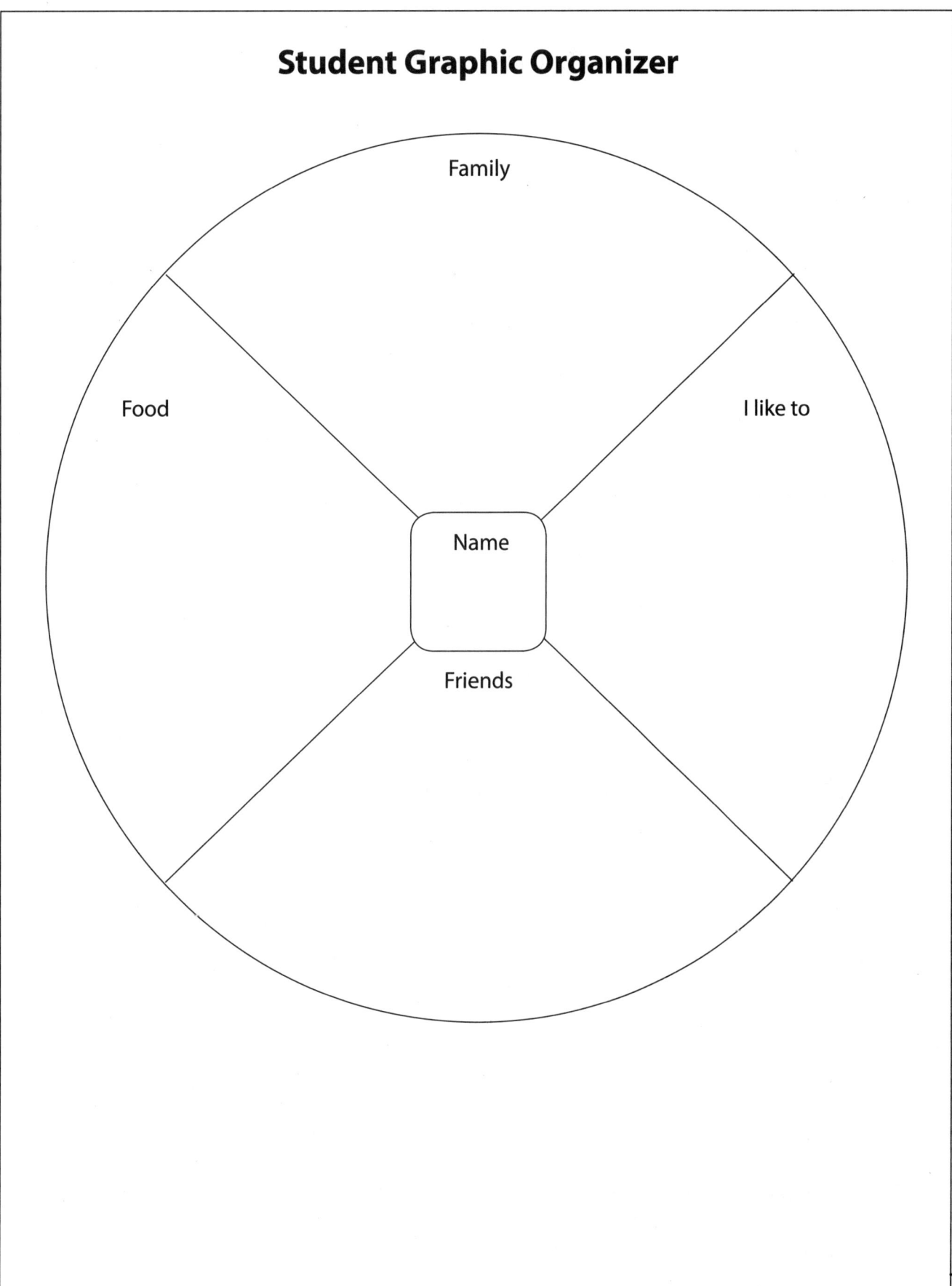

Student Questionnaire: Primary

Date: _____

Dear _____ ,

Please fill out this questionnaire so I can get to know you better.

1. The people in my family are _____.

2. My friends at school are _____.

3. My favorite subject at school is _____.

4. I like to play _____.

5. My favorite sport is _____.

6. I could help my friends _____.

7. I like to eat _____.

Student Questionnaire: Intermediate

Date: _____

Dear _____ ,

Please fill out this questionnaire so I can get to know you better. It will help me to plan topics that you enjoy and want to learn about.

Do you have brothers and sisters? How many? _____

Give their names and ages:

What languages can you speak?

Who are you friends at school?

What makes you feel proud?

What activities are you involved in before and after school?

What do you like most about school?

What do you like the least about school?

What could you help others do?

How could others help you?

If you could travel anywhere, where would you go?

Finish these sentences:

I can learn when _____.

I am a person who _____.

3
The Classroom Community

When you develop community in the classroom, you provide your students with a safe, secure environment where they can freely learn more about themselves and grow in their knowledge and skills. As their teacher, you model caring, acceptance, and support for everyone in the classroom. Through listening to the language of acceptance and modeling inclusion, you show children how to positively function within their community. As teachers, we want to build a community of learners who are proficient in looking after themselves and others. We need to encourage our students to connect with their peers and teachers in meaningful, real-life situations to prepare them for a lifetime of working with others.

Teresa Shume, PhD, Department of Biosciences, Minnesota State University Moorhead, feels her role as a teacher is to establish a community with supports, guidance, and scaffolding that provide meaning to her students. These connections deepen student understanding, and develop proficient, valuable skills as students grow as individuals and community members.

> I belong to Parents Supporting Parents, a group of moms who meet monthly to support each other in bringing up our special-needs children. At a recent meeting, one of the moms explained how her 18-month-old grandson, in a matter of ten days, learned how to wipe his aunt's mouth with a cloth when her face was wet. He also helped get her ready to go out for a car ride by trying to swing out the footrests on her wheelchair and patting her legs in an attempt to help her transfer from her indoor chair to her outdoor chair. Then he would turn to push the elevator button and wait for the click to sound before the door opened. With his family's support, this child got to feel he was playing an important part in getting his aunt prepared to go out. Children of any age can develop their desire and skills to help others when they are shown how to be accepting, tolerant, and respectful by the adults in their lives.

When you put students in group situations they learn to work cooperatively with their peers. You need to do a lot of scaffolding first so students know the steps to take in order to collaborate with each other to produce a group project. In a cooperative science activity, we divided students into five groups according to their strengths and needs. We worked on developing understanding around new science concepts. Each group had a leader, recorder, time-keeper, errand monitor, and presenter. Points were given to each group for how effectively their group worked. Students stayed involved and interested in their work and learned a lot about science. Everyone enjoyed earning points as a group because the points could be cashed in later for more computer time or a longer recess. It was a chance for students to work cooperatively together in their group roles, and groupings were regularly changed so all students had an opportunity to work with everyone.

Students will continue to follow classroom rules and use the boundaries established (see Chapter 2) while working with their peers in group situations. Some students choose to work on their own because they lack the emotional skills or interest needed to work with others. Other students are born directors and further develop their leadership gifts. Group learning prepares students to be able to work effectively with others in their community now and as they get older. Everyone can have a chance to lead their group. I remember working in a Grade 5 classroom in which groups were led by students who had weaker academic skills; however, they were given a lot of supports to help them lead their groups. It was inspirational to see these students successfully take the lead and their group members supporting them. Everyone can be a leader with the right supports.

When you plan together with your students, you end up getting deeper learning and enjoyment out of each teaching situation. Our Grade 7/8 students went to the Festival du Voyageur, a winter festival celebration of history, culture, and *bon ami*. All students attended many creative workshops during the day, but my student group had some free time in the morning before attending back-to-back cultural sessions in the afternoon. We decided as a group to use that free time to visit the store and order special French delicacies to eat. We stayed together to shop and to eat French pastries together. At the end of the day students were happy they had time to visit the store and order tasty food. Students in other groups didn't stay together in their free time and missed out on shopping, eating, and, in some cases, getting to their planned cultural sessions on time. Our group made a plan, enjoyed our time together, and got to all our cultural sessions.

Moral Intelligences

There are several strategies you can use to connect your students' social and emotional learning with their academics; one approach is to base these strategies on moral intelligences.

- Children connect their curriculum knowledge with their life experiences as they use the moral intelligences in all their subjects. I worked at a school that used moral intelligences to guide all students, staff, and parents in developing a supportive learning community. We had constant discussions about what it meant to be kind, respectful, empathetic, fair, and tolerant, to display self-control and use our conscience.
- Through using a communal language of moral intelligences, we help students develop their social, emotional, and academic skills. Language makes the connection from hearing an idea to acting it out in our conversations, writing, and daily connections with others. Moral intelligences can weave perfectly into the values of your school community when everyone uses the same language to teach students about respect, empathy, kindness, and tolerance.
- Moral intelligences can be taught across the curriculum because they tie into curriculum goals.
- In developing these intelligences, the child becomes aware of and begins to demonstrate social responsibility. This is a constant goal in most curriculums. Working as a community within the classroom creates many solutions to curriculum issues and working-group challenges.
- Moral intelligences lead us to celebrate all the treasures in our community because we take time to get to know our peers, where they come from, what's important to them, and how we are all alike, and also to develop appreciation for our diversity.

Michele Borba (2001) outlined the need for developing the moral intelligences of kindness, respect, empathy, fairness, self-control, tolerance, and conscience. These seven virtues help children handle the daily challenges and pressures they will face throughout life.

In my years of working at a K-to-5/6 school, I found that students and their families, as well as school staff, understood what these terms meant. In our school community, families came from more than 40 different countries around the world. The virtues represented by Moral Intelligences tied into their own personal faiths and beliefs. As a school community we took time to teach our students and their families why they were core virtues in our school and how they were engrained in our daily teaching.

Kindness

Kindness is caring about the happiness and feelings of others, and caring for people when they need your help. It can be demonstrated by recognizing the presence of another person, using such actions as smiling, welcoming them, holding the door open for them, tucking their chair in when they sit down. As teachers, we model kindness to our students when we greet them first thing in the morning, after lunch, and after they return to class from other classes with a warm smile. We model kindness by checking to see how they are feeling and if they need extra words of encouragement. These actions let our students know that we care about them and are happy to see them.

See page 43 for the Kindness Class Activity in chart form.

Our next step is to let students know that we expect them to greet us and others in the same way. When visitors would come to our school they would remark at the kindness and respect our students demonstrated. They said they felt welcomed when a student gave a cheery "Hi," opened the door for them, and asked if the visitor needed any help. Our Grade 7 and 8 students were trained to answer the phone in the office over the lunch hour. They would practice a script of how to answer the phone, what a reasonable answer would sound like, and how to use the PA system so they could call staff to the office for a phone call. The students learned how to write up a phone message and how to deliver it to a staff mailbox or to a student in class.

Kindness Class Activity

Teacher-directed

1. Write *Kindness* on the board.
   - Brainstorm with class: What does kindness look like?

Group Work

2. Review what kindness looks like (a smile, opening a door for someone) and sounds like (*Hello; Can I help?; Would you like to play?*).
   - Discuss: What can they do at recess to practice kindness? (invite other students to play; gather students together to organize a game)
   - As a class, make a plan for recess. Go out to practice.
3. Gather together after recess. Write down what was observed at recess.
   - Ask: *Have you learned anything from this recess? Would you do anything differently?*
   - As a class, plan for the next recess. Use the Kindness student worksheet on page 44, with each student having a copy.

Extension Activities

4. Continue making plans for recess until everyone is comfortable that they understand *kindness*.

See page 44 for the Kindness student worksheet; adapt this template according to your students' needs and understanding.

- Make a list of books on kindness for students; include as many as you can in the class library.
- Small-group work: Each group chooses to design a poster, write a story, or write a play to show their understanding of kindness; groups share their work with the class.
- Community projects: Look at safety in the community; gather acts of kindness in the community; practice acts of kindness in the community.

Respect

Respect is valuing others and what is important to them, appreciating the person and everything about him/her. We honor others in how we greet them, in how we carry on our conversations with them, and in our general feelings toward them. Polite language is used in our conversations, and we take the time to listen so we support their thoughts and ideas. We understand they deserve to be treated in an honorable way.

Respect is a virtue that children are taught from the moment they are born. Their parents guide them in valuing others and show how these actions are important to us. Students will have a lot of thoughts, ideas, and experiences around respect before they get to school. You might ask Grade 5 and 6 students to interview students in the various grade levels to find out what respect means to them and then discuss any similarities and differences with the various grade levels. It can give students further insight into what respect looks and sounds like to others.

See page 45 for the Respect Class Activity in chart form.

> A friendship group was formed for J to help strengthen her social skills so she could learn how to play with her friends. She met with her peer group during morning recess. Everyone decided at the beginning of each recess to either draw with sidewalk chalk or use bubble solution to blow bubbles together on the playground. Students were given the language and social prompts to use in helping J become involved in group play. Through this daily experience, J developed her ability to have conversations and play cooperatively with her peers. Instead of playing *alongside* her peers she learned how to play *with* them. Her peers also learned the language needed to encourage and include J in their play. The students showed respect toward each other by listening when someone else was talking, using welcoming language with each other, and watching to see that J was comfortable, happy, and getting a turn to use the recess toys.

Respect Class Activity

Teacher-directed

1. Write *Respect* on the board.
   - Brainstorm with class: What does respect look like?
   - Have a student look up *respect* in the dictionary.

Group Work

2. Review what respect looks and sounds like (saying please and thank you; making sure everyone gets a turn; *Can I help you?*).
   - Discuss: What can they do in the classroom to practice respect? (stand aside while others enter the door; help around the classroom; clean their desks when they are finished; hand in their work on time)
   - As a class, make a plan for demonstrating respect in the classroom.

	3. Gather together and share what respect looked and sounded like.
	• Make a plan for recess. Ask: *What would this look like?*
	• As a class, plan to demonstrate respect at recess. Use the Respect student worksheet on page 46, with each student having a copy.
Extension Activities	4. Continue making plans for recess until everyone is comfortable that they understand *respect*.
	• Make a list of books on respect for students; include as many as you can in the class library.
	• Small-group work: Each group chooses to design a poster, write a story, or write a play to show their understanding of respect; groups share their work with the class.
See page 46 for the Respect student worksheet; adapt this template according to your students' needs and understanding.	• Invite parents to discuss: Do their children demonstrate respect at home and in the community? How?
	• Assembly presentation: The Many Ways of Showing Respect at Our School.

Empathy

Empathy is being able to understand what another person is feeling; being able to put yourself into another person's shoes and understand what their life is like. When students show empathy, they are becoming aware of different points of view, opinions, and ideas; over time students will build compassion and understanding for others.

See page 47 for the Empathy Class Activity in chart form.

Empathy Class Activity

Teacher-directed	1. Write *Empathy* on the board.
	• Brainstorm with class: What does empathy look like?
	• Have a student look up *empathy* in the dictionary.
Individual Work	2. Review what empathy looks and sounds like (relating another's feelings and experiences to your own; *You must be tired walking to the bus stop; when I walked that far I got tired too; You must be sad you lost your bike*).
	• Discuss: What can they do in the classroom to show empathy? How can we put ourselves "in each other's shoes"?
	• Every student traces his/her foot on a piece of paper, then draws and writes what is important and challenging to him/her on the foot. Students gather in groups and share their footprints with their group.
Group Work	3. Gather together and share what empathy looked and sounded like.
	• Each group posts their footprints in a special area in class, or on the board or interactive whiteboard.
	• Each group introduces their members' footprints to the class.
Extension Activities	4. Students take a "walk" as they follow the footprints of a group.
	• Two groups share footprints.
	• Make a list of books on empathy for students; include as many as you can in the class library.
See page 48 for the Empathy student worksheet; adapt this template according to your students' needs and understanding.	• Small-group work: Each group chooses to design a poster, write a story, or write a play to show their understanding of empathy; groups share their work with the class.

> A friendship group met regularly to support a student who used a wheelchair to be mobile. For morning recess the group went to the gym, making a point to walk alongside W. Once there, students formed two teams and played broomball, with an emphasis on making sure the ball got passed to W. They also encouraged him to swing at the ball with his broom. Everyone wanted their turn on W's team. We all tried to keep the game moving fast so the students' interest level was high; an adult moved with W to make sure he would know what it felt like to play the game actively. When our school physiotherapist offered to help us organize a wheelchair obstacle course for Grade 3–6 classes, W's friendship group jumped at the opportunity. Every ambulatory participant had a turn to move through the obstacle course in a borrowed wheelchair. We developed a video of the Obstacle Experience and shared it during a whole-school assembly to emphasize sharing and getting along, and to show everyone how much fun we had.

Fairness

See page 49 for the Fairness Class Activity in chart form.

Fairness is treating people with equality and justice. When students are taught fairness, the atmosphere in our playgrounds, classrooms, families, and community improves; students can see that this trumps being the best or earning the most. Fairness can be as simple as showing another person that, now that you have had a turn, you want them to have their turn. It can be wanting to share your food, toys, and time with another person; i.e., you know you have something, so you take the time to make sure your friends have something too. Deciding to study for a test instead of cheating, and congratulating the winning team even though it hurts to lose are further examples of being fair. Students need to be taught fairness as young children and to be encouraged by mentors who demonstrate through their actions how to be fair. That way, they learn to stand up for what is right, not for what is the easiest to do.

> In a school project that had students working on fairness and respect, the class built a human-like body made from clear packing tape to show the inner-workings of the circulatory system. This project was cross-curricular, including English language arts, science, health, art, and drama. Students planned how to work through the project cooperatively so that everyone had a turn in developing the packing-tape person. Students observed who had a turn and who would be next to wrap the plastic around another student's body part to form parts of the model. They all worked with their teacher to put the plastic person together and place the circulatory system inside. Everyone made sure that everyone else had a turn helping to create the transparent human body. It became all of the students' responsibility to make sure that everyone had a turn to ensure fairness for everyone.

Fairness Class Activity

Teacher-directed

1. Write *Fairness* on the board.
   - Brainstorm with class: What does fairness look like?
   - Have a student look up *fairness* in the dictionary.

Group Work

2. Review what fairness looks and sounds like (making sure everyone gets a turn; sharing things equally; *We tossed a coin and you chose heads; it's your turn*).
   - Discuss: What can they do in the classroom to show fairness?
   - Students gather in groups to share what fairness looks and sounds like.
3. Gather together as a class and share what fairness looks and sounds like.
   - Each group acts out scenarios to show fairness.
   - Each group shares their fairness scenarios with the class.

Extension Activities

4. Each group chooses to design a poster, write a story, or write a play about fairness on the playground to show their understanding of respect; groups share their work with the teacher.
   - Make a list of books on fairness for students; include as many as you can in the class library.
   - Groups write a scenario about fairness in sports, music, friendships, or preparing for tests.
   - Read a story, put on a play, or share a poster with other classes.

See page 50 for the Fairness student worksheet; adapt this template according to your students' needs and understanding.

Self-Control

See page 51 for the Self-Control Class Activity in chart form.

Self-control is the ability to manage your own feelings and behavior, regulating your emotions so you can do what is right in a situation. It can be waiting for your turn, sharing the last cookie with your friend instead of eating it all yourself, not shouting at a friend when you have lost a game. You have the ability to stop and think before you act. When you are using self-control, you are choosing to act in a positive way.

Discussing self-control opens the door to talking about how everyone has different abilities to handle stress and their emotions. You can talk about how some students are naturally more emotional and quick to react, while others stop first and think before they act. It can be helpful for students to look at themselves and see how they react in situations, but only if this can be handled in a non-threatening way so nobody puts a value on how each student reacts. You need to set up clear parameters around discussing students' abilities to handle their emotions. Time needs to be invested in developing a working relationship with students in which students feel enough trust in the group to talk about themselves. Take these steps slowly and move forward only as fast as your students are able to handle group and personal discussions. Collaborate with guidance/resource teachers for ideas and support so you have another adult monitoring the class growth. As the classroom teacher, you have the whole year to model and discuss self-control.

A handful of students from a combined Grade 1/2/3 classroom were having trouble getting along. Sometimes they played cooperatively at recess, but most times several students in the group would decide on their own to change the playing rules and a fight would break out. The students and I decided to meet every other day for 30 minutes. As a group we read stories, talked about recess play situations, and discussed how respect and self-control played an important part in everybody getting along. Over time, the students started understanding how to use their language positively and effectively while playing with their peers at recess and interacting together in the classroom. They were able to practice being cooperative and listening to their peers. They became noticeably happier and had fewer

> instances of getting angry and upset with each other. They learned that using self-control leads to positive play with their peers, that stopping and thinking before you act helps the group make better decisions.

Self-Control Class Activity

Teacher-directed

1. Write *Self-control* on the board.
   - Brainstorm with class: What does self-control look like?
   - Have a student look up *self-control* in the dictionary.

Group Work

2. Review what self-control looks and sounds like (waiting before reacting; waiting for your turn; *I want the cookie but there is only one left, so you can have it; When you yell at me, instead of yelling back, I will walk away*).
   - Discuss: What can they do in the classroom to show self-control?
   - Students gather in groups to share what self-control looks and sounds like.
3. Gather together as a class and share what self-control looks and sounds like.
   - Each group draws a poster about how they use self-control at school.
   - Each group shares their self-control poster with the class.

Extension Activities

4. Each group writes a story or a play about self-control at school to show their understanding of self-control; groups share their plans with the teacher.
   - Make a list of books on self-control for students; include as many as you can in the class library.
   - Invite parents to school so students can share their Highlights of Self-Control.
   - Read a story or put on a play for other classes showing what you understand about self-control.

See page 52 for the Self-Control student worksheet; adapt this template according to your students' needs and understanding.

Tolerance

See page 53 for the Tolerance Class Activity in chart form.

Tolerance is showing that you accept others as they are. Other people may have similarities to, as well as differences from, you. Showing tolerance means you appreciate and respect their uniqueness. Another person's ethnicity, religious beliefs, economic status, and/or sexual preferences do not stand in your way of treating them respectfully.

For children to talk about tolerance, time must be invested in ensuring they feel safe in their classroom, that they trust their teacher and peers to not disrespect their thoughts and ideas. You need to prepare students for these discussions. Keep examples simple and close to their daily lives before working up to larger issues like ethnicity and sexuality. Following the grade curriculum can help guide you through these topics.

> Three Grade 3 students were talking and invited me into their conversation. They proceeded to tell me how they were from different parts of the world. They explained that the way each of them honored their God was by having the name of their God in their family name. The students were comfortable talking about this, and with pride and excitement. It was important to them and they wanted to share. I marvelled at how well the boys got along and enjoyed working together in class on a group presentation. Back in the countries they had emigrated from, their ethnic identities would not tolerate a positive connection between these boys. They were fortunate enough to find themselves living in a country that values tolerance and acceptance of diversity.

Teacher-directed

Individual Work

Group Work

Extension Activities

See page 54 for the Tolerance student worksheet; adapt this template according to your students' needs and understanding.

Tolerance Class Activity

1. Write *Tolerance* on the board.
   - Brainstorm with class: What does tolerance look like?
   - Have a student look up *tolerance* in the dictionary.
2. Review what tolerance looks and sounds like (making accommodations for different abilities; *I will stop the movie when my friend with ADHD needs a movement break; I will wait for my friend to answer because he/she is slower at processing a question*).
   - Have students think about what they can do in the classroom to show tolerance.
   - If students feel safe and listened to enough to open up, they share what tolerance looks and sounds like.
3. Gather together as a class and share what tolerance looks and sounds like.
   - Each group acts out scenarios to show what tolerance looks like in the community.
   - Each group shares their tolerance scenarios with the class.
4. Invite community health agencies to the classroom to talk about mental health issues and conditions; e.g., depression, anxiety, autism, etc.
   - Classrooms discuss having visitors and prepare questions to ask the presenter.
   - Make a list of books on tolerance for students; include as many as you can in the class library.

Conscience

Conscience is knowing the difference between a right decision and a wrong decision; it is the inner voice that tells you if you have made a good choice. Over time your parents, teachers, and friends teach you how to make the right choices in life; every day you are practicing how to do this. As you get older, you understand and accept the rules of your family and community. These rules become your rules, and your conscience reminds you to follow them.

Students are regularly faced with making decisions about how to handle responsibilities both inside and outside the classroom. It's important to have conversations with them about what a right or wrong decision looks like and what the expectations are when they have special responsibilities; e.g., as a classroom helper. The more conversations students have regarding right and wrong, the better prepared they will be for making decisions.

See page 55 for the Conscience Class Activity in chart form.

- What do you do when you want something but know it doesn't belong to you?
- Why is it important to always be honest with yourself and others?
- How do you handle friends who make poor choices? Are you going to be a follower?
- Is there a way to leave the situation with your dignity intact?

These are good conversations for students to have because it prepares them for how to act when they are on their own or with a group of students. Trust and honesty are emphasized as goals that students want to achieve.

> I have worked with older students, both posting and on the receiving end of negative Internet comments. Whenever students post negative comments about another student, they need to be aware they are sharing their negative thoughts with the whole world, leaving the victim vulnerable to criticism and further hurtful posts. As most students are using cell phones, negative posts are not seen by the school or teacher until the victim or other students bring it to their attention. These posts need to be taken seriously; teachers need to act swiftly to address the problem with administration and students. It's important to take time to get all of the details and sit down with the victim and offender to find solutions. Parents need to be included in the details and discussions so the problem is dealt with and resolved. In extreme cases, police might be involved.

Conscience Class Activity

Teacher-directed

1. Write *Conscience* on the board.
   - Brainstorm with class: What does conscience look like?
   - Have a student look up *conscience* in the dictionary.

Individual Work

2. Review what conscience looks and sounds like (feeling bad about a wrong decision you've made; knowing that a friend is making a wrong decision; *I am not going to copy my friend's answers on the test because it is wrong*; *If you are stealing candy, I will not go to the store with you*).
   - Have students think about what they can do in the classroom to show conscience.
   - Students gather in groups to share what conscience looks and sounds like.

Group Work

3. Gather together as a class and share what conscience looks and sounds like.
   - Each group acts out scenarios to show what conscience looks like in the community.
   - Each group shares their conscience scenarios with the class.

Extension Activities

4. Groups choose to draw a poster, or write a story or play about conscience in the community; groups share their plans with the teacher.
   - Read a story, put on a play, or share a poster with other classes.
   - Make a list of books on conscience for students; include as many as you can in the class library.

See page 56 for the Conscience student worksheet; adapt this template according to your students' needs and understanding.

Kindness Class Activity

	Introduce/Review	Discuss	Plan
1. Teacher-directed	Write *Kindness* on the board.	Brainstorm: *What does kindness look like? Sound like?*	
2. Group Work	Review what kindness looks and sounds like.	What can students do at recess to practice kindness?	As a class, make a plan for recess.
3. Group Work	Gather as a class; write observations from recess.	Ask: *Have you learned anything from this recess? Would you do anything differently?*	As a class, plan for next recess.
4. Extension Activities	Make a list of books on kindness for students; include as many as you can in the class library.	Small-group work: Each group chooses to design a poster, write a story, or write a play to show their understanding of kindness; groups share their work with the class.	Community projects: Look at safety in the community; gather acts of kindness in the community; practice acts of kindness in the community.

Kindness

Date: _____   Name: _____

Group Members	
Kindness sounds like…	
Kindness looks like…	
Recess Plan	
What did I observe at recess?	
Did I learn anything from this recess?	
Next time, I would…	
Plan for next recess	

Respect Class Activity

	Introduce/Review	Discuss	Plan/Share
1. Teacher-directed	Write *Respect* on the board.	Brainstorm: *What does respect look like? Sound like?*	Have a student look up *respect* in the dictionary.
2. Group Work	Review what respect looks and sounds like.	What can students do in the classroom to practice respect?	As a class, make a plan for demonstrating respect in the classroom.
3. Group Work	Gather as a class; share what respect looks and sounds like.	Share what respect looked and sounded like in the classroom.	As a class, plan to demonstrate respect at recess.
4. Extension Activities	• Make a list of books on respect for students; include as many as you can in the class library. • Invite parents to discuss: *Do their children demonstrate respect at home and in the community? How?*	Small-group work: Each group chooses to design a poster, write a story, or write a play to show their understanding of respect; groups share their work with the class.	Assembly presentation: The Many Ways of Showing Respect at Our School.

Respect

Date: _____   Name: _____

Group Members	
Respect looks and sounds like…	
How to practice respect in the classroom	
What did I observe?	
Recess Plan	
Did I learn anything from this recess?	
Next time, I would…	

Empathy Class Activity

	Introduce/Review	Discuss	Plan/Share
1. Teacher-directed	Write *Empathy* on the board.	Brainstorm: *What does empathy look like? Sound like?*	Have a student look up *empathy* in the dictionary.
2. Group Work	Review what empathy looks and sounds like.	What can students do in the classroom to show empathy?	In groups, students create footprints to show what is important and challenging to them.
3. Group Work	Gather as a class; share what empathy looks and sounds like.	Each group posts their footprints and introduces them to the class.	Students follow the footprints of a group to "walk in another's footprints."
4. Extension Activities	Make a list of books on empathy for students; include as many as you can in the class library.	Two groups share footprints.	Small-group work: Each group chooses to design a poster, write a story, or write a play to show their understanding of empathy; groups share their work with the class.

Empathy

Date: _____   Name: _____

Group Members	
Empathy sounds like…	
Empathy looks like…	
How to show empathy in the classroom	
What did I share that was important to me?	
What did I learn was important to others?	
Next time, I would…	

Fairness Class Activity

	Introduce/Review	Discuss	Plan/Share
1. Teacher-directed	Write *Fairness* on the board.	Brainstorm: *What does fairness look like? Sound like?*	Have a student look up *fairness* in the dictionary.
2. Group Work	Review what fairness looks and sounds like.	What can students do in the classroom to show fairness?	In groups, students share what fairness would look and sound like in the classroom.
3. Group Work	Gather as a class; share what fairness looks and sounds like.	Each group acts out scenarios to show fairness.	Groups share their fairness scenarios with the class.
4. Extension Activities	Make a list of books on fairness for students; include as many as you can in the class library.	Groups write a scenario about fairness in sports, in music, friendships, or in preparing for tests.	Students read a story, put on a play, or share a poster with other classes.

Fairness

Date: _____ Name: _____

Group Members	
Fairness sounds like…	
Fairness looks like…	
Fairness scenarios	
What did I observe watching other groups' scenarios?	
Next time, I would…	
How to show fairness on the playground	

Self-Control Class Activity

	Introduce/Review	Discuss	Plan/Share
1. Teacher-directed	Write *Self-control* on the board.	Brainstorm: *What does self-control look like? Sound like?*	Have a student look up *self-control* in the dictionary.
2. Group Work	Review what self-control looks and sounds like.	What can students do in the classroom to show self-control?	In groups, students share what self-control would look and sound like in the classroom.
3. Group Work	Gather as a class; share what self-control looks and sounds like.	Each group draws a poster about how they use self-control at school.	Groups share their self-control posters with the class.
4. Extension Activities	Make a list of books on self-control for students; include as many as you can in the class library.	Groups write a story or play about self-control at school; groups share their plans with the teacher.	• Invite parents to school so students can share their Highlights of Self-control. • Students read a story or put on a play for other classes showing understanding of self-control.

Self-Control

Date: _____   Name: _____

Group Members	
Self-control sounds like…	
Self-control looks like…	
How to show self-control at school	
Poster Plan	
What I observed about other posters	
Next time, I would…	
How to show self-control on the playground	

Tolerance Class Activity

	Introduce/Review	Discuss	Plan/Share
1. Teacher-directed	Write *Tolerance* on the board.	Brainstorm: *What does tolerance look like? Sound like?*	Have a student look up *tolerance* in the dictionary.
2. Group Work	Review what tolerance looks and sounds like.	Students think about what can they do in the classroom to show tolerance.	If students feel safe, they share what tolerance looks and sounds like from their experience.
3. Group Work	Gather as a class; share what tolerance looks and sounds like.	Each group acts out scenarios to show what tolerance looks like in the community.	Groups share their tolerance scenarios with the class.
4. Extension Activities	Make a list of books on tolerance for students; include as many as you can in the class library.	Invite community health agencies to the classroom to talk about mental health issues and conditions.	Classrooms discuss having visitors and prepare questions to ask the presenter.

Tolerance

Date: _____ Name: _____

Group Members	
Tolerance sounds like…	
Tolerance looks like…	
Things that are difficult for me	
How to show tolerance in the community	
What I observed about scenarios	
Next time, I would…	
Do I need more information? Questions for presenters	

Conscience Class Activity

	Introduce/Review	Discuss	Plan/Share
1. Teacher-directed	Write *Conscience* on the board.	Brainstorm: *What does conscience look like? Sound like?*	Have a student look up *conscience* in the dictionary.
2. Group Work	Review what conscience looks and sounds like.	What can students do in the classroom to show conscience?	In groups, students share what conscience looks and sounds like.
3. Group Work	Gather as a class; share what conscience looks and sounds like.	Each group acts out scenarios to show what conscience looks like in the community.	Groups share their conscience scenarios with the class.
4. Extension Activities	Make a list of books on conscience for students; include as many as you can in the class library.	Groups write a story or play about conscience in the community; groups share their plans with the teacher.	Students read a story, put on a play, or share a poster about conscience with other classes.

Conscience

Date: _____   Name: _____

Group Members	
Conscience sounds like…	
Conscience looks like…	
How to practice conscience in the classroom	
Community Plan	
What I observed in the community	
Did I learn anything?	
Next time, I would…	

4

The Responsive Classroom

The Responsive Classroom is not a curriculum, but an approach to teaching that places an emphasis on the academic, social, and emotional growth of children within a supportive school community. Academic success is strongly tied to building social-emotional competencies. This approach works well in establishing the foundation for developing the moral intelligences of kindness, respect, empathy, fairness, self-control, tolerance, and conscience in our students.

A responsive classroom is connected to student interests, is interactive, is challenging, and is built around purposeful tasks. Teachers nurture belonging and safety, so students are comfortable taking risks and working with their peers. The classroom environment is calm and focused on learning, and students are encouraged to be independent. Teachers use daily observations to develop an appropriate learning environment and individualize programs as necessary.

The guiding principles of a responsive classroom include the belief that the social and emotional curriculum is just as important as the academic curriculum. How children learn new information is just as important as what they learn. Social interaction ensures great cognitive growth. To be successful, students need to learn the set of social and emotional skills defined as moral intelligences. These skills tie in with getting to know students and their families, and understanding what it's like to walk in their shoes. In the school community, all adults need to support each other and work as a positive team with students and families.

For example, by working with a group of Grade 2 students in a friendship group, I was able to help them develop skills so they could show respect and empathy toward each other when they played together at recess. They were able to play at recess without deciding to change the rules in the middle of the game. The students knew that they had to continue with the rules they agreed upon at the start of the game and keep this going until the end; for students, that became the right decision to make.

Sample Strategies for the Responsive Classroom

The Language of Community

What would a K–8 responsive classroom school look like? The teacher's language is a positive and powerful teaching tool. To positively connect with our students we need to show we care for and respect them.

Positive comments must be specific and not just general praise, because students need to know details of how they did well in their work and behavior. When we give students direction, we need to be directive, not simply suggest they act a certain way. Students will respond immediately if they have been taught that when a request is given they need to act upon it. When we redirect our students, we should be clear and specific, so students know what they need to do. We need to keep value judgments out of our comments.

It is important to have daily discussions with students to confirm understanding of new concepts and then check to see if this new information fits with their own understanding. It gives students a voice to say if the new information makes sense to them. For example, in a discussion with a group of Grade 7 and 8 students, I found what was most important to them at school. Some of the students had recently immigrated to Canada, were learning English, and continued to have struggles in school. They shared their challenges in learning English. Some were unhappy with their performance on tests and their marks; they had hoped to get higher marks with all their studying. There was a gap in what they had hoped their final marks would be and the effort they put into studying for the test. As a teacher, I found it helpful to have this information to help them close that gap.

One student with a learning disability talked about children who had dyslexia; he was using talk about the topic in general to express his own personal struggles. He felt there was hope that he could be successful. He shared how many astronauts have dyslexia and the reason they were hired was because they knew how to think outside the box; he believed he had that skill too. It was good to know he thought he would be successful. It was important for him to have something he felt he was good at. Learning was exciting for him and he saw the importance of coming to school. This student was receiving extra help in his reading and writing, and the success of this support was showing in the child's improved self-confidence. He could see a future for himself in spite of his learning challenges. Through daily discussions we continue to check the present understanding of our students and where we need to go in our learning so students always move forward in their understanding.

Social Stories

The moral intelligences of kindness, respect, empathy, fairness, self-control, tolerance, and conscience develop each child's social, emotional, and academic skills. The more practice students have with moral intelligences, the better they understand what getting along looks like and the more able they are to practice getting along with their peers and adults in their daily lives. This is done as groups of students and their teacher write social stories, create classroom plays around the intelligences, and invite others to join them in their curriculum learning; students will listen to related library stories and take these stories home to read again with their families.

"Social Stories are a social learning tool that supports the safe and meaningful exchange of information between parents, professionals, and people who are autistic" (Gray, 1991). In my teaching, I have found that social stories are helpful to all students, as they give detailed information based on what needs to be learned and lots of opportunities for discussion and practice.

A social story is a story with pictures that explains how a particular skill is performed. Social stories help bridge the gap between being taught a skill and being able to understand and demonstrate the skill, because rereading the story helps a student better understand the concept each time. Taking actual pictures of the classroom and friends makes the contents more pleasing and interesting to read; students love to see themselves in a story. I have used social stories for students with academic issues other than autism; the social story is a way to con-

For more information on social stories check out CarolGraySocialStories.com

nect these children to their learning. The social stories shown here were written with the help of the student and the classroom teacher and shared with the child's parent. Many team meetings preceded writing the stories so the child, parent, and teacher had input.

Sample Social Stories

Hi, my name is R____
I can make egg salad sandwiches. I wash my hands first.
I have to boil the egg. Then I peel the egg.
I need to mash the eggs.
I add mayonnaise to the eggs.
I toast the bread.
I spread the egg salad on the bread.
I put my sandwich on a plate.
I eat my egg salad sandwich.
I wash my dishes.
I dry my dishes.
I put my dishes away. I am finished.

How to Play with My Friends
Walk up to your friend.
Look into your friend's eyes.
Ask your friend, "Can I play?"
Play with your friend.

My name is _____
I like to take my turn.
I like to be first in line.
Now I'm second in line. I like to take my turn.
Then I'm third in line. That's okay because I'm taking my turn.
Sometimes I have to be last. I'm taking my turn.

> PowerPoint and other presentation tools are great for developing social stories. They can easily accommodate words and pictures, and can be edited at any time. Students can be given copies of their stories to take home and read with their families; a copy is left in the class library.

Pictures and words describing students involved in positive learning experiences have helped to open doors to possibilities. Showing a student step-by-step how to make an egg salad sandwich and how to clean up after eating the sandwich can help the student develop reading skills and see that school experiences can be tasty and positive. Another child will learn how to go up to their friends on the playground and get invited into their play. A student will learn to be okay with being first, second, third, or fourth in line; being first in line won't be their only choice.

The Morning Meeting

> It can be useful to choose a spot by the board or interactive whiteboard with a carpet that students can sit on or an area large enough to put chairs into a circle.

In a responsive classroom, the day begins with the morning meeting (Kriete & Davis, 2014), for which the classroom community is brought together in a circle in the room's meeting area. These meetings provide students daily opportunities to interact with their peers and staff to further develop either emotional and social learning. Academic skills can also be reviewed and practiced during Morning Meeting (Kriete & Davis, 2014).

This daily 20- to 30-minute activity can be arranged in other periods, but it works best first thing in the morning. During the morning meeting, students develop strong cognitive abilities and social and emotional proficiencies. Students develop improved ways to be heard and to listen to their peers; children are given a voice. The meeting sets a respectful tone of trust and engaged learning. It also meets everyone's need to belong and have fun together. The four components of the morning meeting are

- greeting each other
- sharing something important
- a group activity, which can be academic
- looking at the morning message together.

Greeting in alphabetical order is great practice for students just learning English.

> As the Grade 5/6 students entered their class they read the whiteboard to see what they would be sharing that day; every child knew he/she needed to share. That morning the students were left the message *Tell me a family story*. The students started their meeting with greeting their peers in alphabetical order. The teacher would go through the alphabet to cue the students who would be next; that day she started with student names whose names were at the end of the alphabet. A special-needs student was welcomed to the circle and guided by her instructional assistant in welcoming another student. While they were waiting for their turn, the student sat close to her instructional assistant and quietly read a book. After every student received a greeting, students started to share their stories about their families. This experience helped students get to know and better understand each other. Their teacher got to know her students on a personal level, gleaning knowledge about their likes and dislikes.
>
> The class activity involved building a story by adding to it as they moved around the circle. The students' story got as far as *One of my friends had…* when the next student couldn't remember the word in correct sequence, so they had to start the story from the beginning again. This got students to really pay attention to what their neighbor was saying so they could repeat and add another word to the story. The students started to pull together as a team.
>
> The teacher had December's goal written on the board as the morning message: *Kindness with a cause*. Students were collecting money, shovelling snow, visiting seniors, babysitting, and collecting food and mittens to be given away in holiday hampers.

Community Involvement

Through developing moral intelligences, students will become aware of and demonstrate social responsibility; this is a constant goal in many curricula. Students can learn important academic and social skills through taking on community responsibilities.

Crossing Patrols

I led the patrols in my school for more than six years. We worked hard at our daily practice and the learning of new skills was taken seriously. Patrols would meet each morning before their shift to get organized and then go out on post together. We frequently talked about our skills and would practice what patrolling looked like before we got out onto the streets. Each shift had a patrol captain who would walk between posts to encourage patrols and monitor student safety. I would be present to monitor patrols by the school entrances. Each spring, Grade 6 patrols would teach new Grade 5 students the daily protocol of arriving for our patrol shift, making sure they were dressed appropriately for the weather and confident in their method of safely crossing students, and readying the new patrols for the fall.

Goals were set for our patrols by the school division and our provincial insurance company. I found that it was important to combine the knowledge part of our goals with social and emotional goals. As well as learning how to properly cross students, patrols needed to know how to work with a partner, how to listen to direction from their captain, and how to get crossing students to follow their direction. The patrols were providing an important service for the community, so they needed to realize their service would be monitored and reported on by our neighborhood and community police officers.

Our patrols were a community within the larger school community; we had common goals and enjoyed being together. Our goal was to *Be Our Best*. Each year our patrols had a school competition, in which they performed their crossing duties before the discerning eyes of our school community police officer and school administrator. The patrols enjoyed practicing with a partner over recess or during the lunch hour. We had a special lunch during the competition. This was an extra reward our patrols deserved because they took their responsibilities seriously. The patrols worked on their respect, kindness, self-control, and conscience skills.

Students and Seniors Bowling Club

Several of our Grade 5 classrooms bowled with seniors at a personal care home in our school community, a volunteering opportunity organized by our Community Liaison officer. Once a week, we would all walk to the personal-care home to bowl with the seniors. Students got first-hand experience in gently guiding a senior in throwing a bowling ball, in using encouraging words so their senior partners would be pleased with their results, and in being helpful by resetting the bowling pins and having pleasant conversations. The students made the seniors happy and developed more confidence in themselves every time they went to bowl. They continually worked on their empathy, respect, and tolerance skills.

Class Outings

Showing respect and tolerance toward the diversity in our class comes from appreciation of other cultures, abilities, and family life styles. We become a community through noticing, learning from, and appreciating our differences. In developing diversity our school organized our Grade 5 and 6 students to have lunch at a local mosque. The mosque was within walking distance of the school, so we divided our classes into walking groups and arrived at noon. The children enjoyed the vegan food served and went back for seconds. We were given a tour through the area of prayers and given some explanation of ethnic dress. The students felt welcomed and cared for during the tour. Students who regularly attended the mosque were proud to show their peers their place of worship. Many parents of our students volunteered during the lunch and made sure everyone was comfortable and full of great food. Before the visit, teachers took the time to prepare their students and their families for the visit so everyone would be at ease and have a great time. This tour further developed our understanding around being a Muslim and our respect for the beliefs of Islam. Everyone felt richer inside from the visit.

Cross-Curricular Learning

Research by Dr. Sara Rimm-Kaufman (2014) has shown a strong link between academic success and development of social-emotional skills. Working on learning and social-emotional skills together strengthened both and made the skills stronger for longer. The gains were seen across socio-economic lines; even students from poorer areas did well. There were stronger results for students who were initially lower-achieving than others. Academic choice scored high with math and reading achievements; when students could choose the process to show what they learned, they achieved higher marks. There were improved student achievement and teacher–student interactions, and higher quality instructions in mathematics.

Teachers develop goals for the class and then individual student goals by making sure classroom learning connects to the lives of each individual student. We need to show that we have faith that our students can succeed; from this they will try their best to reach the goal set out for them. The goal can be adjusted until finally they arrive at a completed goal. All students can achieve carefully designed learning goals no matter what their abilities.

Curriculum outlines vocabulary that should be introduced for each lesson; it is the job of the teacher and students to connect it to past learning. The child's personal relationship vocabulary can also be stretched in each lesson. Children learn what respect, tolerance, kindness, and empathy mean in connection with their academic vocabulary. Social responsibility is tied to each curriculum unit. The teacher provides opportunities for the child to learn about these concepts, discuss their meaning, and practice what they mean through classroom activities, school projects, and conversations with parents and family.

Provincial curricula list learning goals for all students, and recognize that increased and deeper learning results when students develop their knowledge base through working collaboratively with their peers and teacher. For example, in the Physical Education/Health curriculum, personal skills, interpersonal skills, and critical and creative thinking skills are combined with active and healthy living skills and movement competence. The school curriculum connects with the inner child's need to be active and interact with their peers. Movement education combined with developing interpersonal connecting skills with peers and the enjoyment of playing sports will carry into adulthood.

Children receive further practice in connecting curriculum with their life experiences when moral intelligences are used in all subject areas. When you teach your concepts across the curriculum, you combine your goals and teach them all at the same time. This strategy gives students further connections to help them learn at a deeper level. The more connections students are given, the better they will understand and retain their learning.

Interactive learning gives students opportunities to work in groups with their peers. Through these experiences students learn to work with others, to resolve conflicts, and, in higher grades, become familiar with stress management. Working as a community within the classroom creates many solutions to curriculum issues and working-group challenges.

Sample Lessons

The following lesson samples show teachers teaching students across the curriculum.

Sample Science Lesson

A student teacher introduced a science lesson on how sound is caused by vibrations. Some students rocked back and forth in rockers to help regulate their body; others sat on the carpet while the lesson was introduced. The learning needs of all were accommodated. Every child was attentive and focused on the lesson details and instructions.

The science lesson goals included helping students to positively work together to solve a science mystery, and lesson preparation supported this. Students had learned to stop their work and pay attention to their student teacher and/or classroom teacher when a chime was rung; a smaller group of students had training the day before to be group leaders. There were four stations: Water, Rubber Band, Dancing Salt, and Ping Pong Ball stations. The student teacher had all materials ready in each centre and did an excellent job explaining the centres to the students. To ensure that all students could follow through with the directions, she placed a specially trained student in each centre to explain how to move from one centre to another. To complete observation sheets for every centre, students had to decide who would write the information.

Students knew how to use the materials in each centre but they didn't know what they would see when they followed the instructions. Amazement was visible on the children's faces when they combined a tuning fork with a ping pong ball, water, and salt; they heard different pitches after plucking rubber bands over a coffee container.

Being able to complete a science experiment as a group goes hand-in-hand with knowing how to cooperate, listen to others, and share. Students need all these skills in order to successfully complete a group experiment. Working in a group provides discussion, reflection, turn-taking, problem-solving, and coming to a consensus.

Through the sample lessons, students demonstrated kindness and respect toward their teacher and fellow students. They were willing to get involved and experiment with the lesson materials, to try them out and learn to feel what learning is all about. They practiced fairness with their peers and teacher and made sure everyone got a chance. They showed self-control by waiting for their turn, not talking while others were talking, and saying only positive things during the lesson. The students were tolerant of their peers and did not make fun of their work or how they spoke. They offered supportive comments to help relax their friends as they were giving a presentation or sharing an idea. They used their consciences while writing a test by not trying to get help from their friends.

Sample Language Arts Lesson

A Grade 5/6 lesson had students develop the beginning, middle, and end of a graphic novel. The student teacher prepared graphic organizers to help students organize and develop their story lines. Their first graphic organizer was on 11" × 17" paper so students had lots of room to write the beginning, middle, and ending of their story. They could transfer their information to a smaller graphic organizer or get into writing the beginning of their story. I noticed lots of students would go back to the larger graphic organizer to remind them of their initial story thoughts.

In this science experiment, the teacher shared a story about a group leader. This boy had come to class the year before afraid to talk and reluctant to get involved with his peers in class. Working on the group experiment helped this student become confident in being a leader, helping his team, writing experiment results, and/or sharing information with the rest of the class.

> Activities were adapted for students with fewer writing skills: they could draw a picture to visualize their thoughts and add a few sentences in a picture bubble to highlight their thoughts; they drew the beginning, middle, and end as three pictures.

Prior to the story all students had chosen "a moment in space" to base their story on. The teacher chunked the lesson information into meaningful pieces and supported this with presentations on the interactive whiteboard on the structure of a story. While students worked at their desks they could ask peers for advice and question the teacher as she moved around the class to assist students in their writing. Writing was a whole-class effort, as everyone pored over their graphic organizers and transferred ideas to their story. Educational assistants sat with a group of students who needed more assistance in their writing to complete their adapted writing activity. When students were finished writing their stories, they partnered with another student who had finished writing and gathered on the carpet. Partners helped each other reflect on whether their stories made sense and made suggestions for possible changes.

The teacher did an excellent job of developing a writing community within her classroom. She knew how to inform her students by providing lots of visual information and hands-on writing tools. Students were well-prepared to write their graphic novels. There were abundant opportunities to share their thoughts with their teacher and peers through the writing process. This was an interactive community writing project.

Sample Math Lesson

A student teacher got her whole class involved in a math lesson on reflections. She opened her lesson by putting on the interactive whiteboard a picture of an ambulance with *Ambulance* written backward. She asked her students, "Why are the letters backward?" Students were immediately drawn into the question. She said she knew it would be difficult for students, since they weren't drivers yet, but what could they use in the car to help them see this?

Students took turns being a driver by standing in front of the picture and holding a mirror to read what was on the front of the ambulance. Students were drawn into past lessons as they talked about reflections and defined *flipped* as another word they used for a reflection. With the use of a mirror they learned about *the line of reflection*, and each student got a mirror to practice showing what a reflected shape looked like and completed an activity at his/her desk. The teacher encouraged everyone to try their best (even if they found it frustrating).

> Academic choice must be present in responsive classrooms because it allows students to have more autonomy around when and how they show their understanding of new concepts. Research shows that with academic choice, children have few behavioral challenges in their learning.

Through the lesson, the teacher created a group dynamic in which all her students were drawn into understanding reflections. Using pointed questions, exciting shapes on the interactive whiteboard, and useful tools (a mirror), she allowed each student to experiment with and understand the line of reflection. Students worked in groups and supported each other as their teacher worked from the front of the class and moved through the groups to support students as they completed their activities.

5

Taking Relationships Home

> Parents are key members of the child's support team and they should always feel welcomed and respected. We may not use everything they suggest, but a collaborative relationship means they will accept that their ideas can't always be used in class.

When I first started teaching, I found connecting with the parents of my students a daunting task. I would always find talking about their child's strengths easy but delving into a student's learning needs was difficult. I was nervous about getting to the point; our conversation would get sidetracked and then it would be over. I found that it helped when I took the time to have daily conversations with parents as they dropped their child off at school or picked them up when school was over. Our conversations, over time, become reciprocal as we end up sharing ideas back and forth. When a friendship with a parent starts to get comfortable, I like to share information about myself. In this relaxed context, I feel I can start talking more specifically about their child. Has the parent thought about challenging the child with a new hobby? Are there things the parent fails to see that are positive about how the child can share with others? Would the parent be willing to read with the child each evening with class library books? It's a lot easier to get to the point with parents when they are comfortable talking to you.

Over the years I have learned a lot and received tremendous support from my students' parents. I still treasure a note that a parent gave me at the end of my first year of teaching. This father was congratulating me on our hands-on program and encouraging me to continue this in the future. He told me to be brave and believe in what I was doing. Over the years I have had the honor and pleasure of working with hundreds of supportive and knowledgeable parents who have taught me many important things. My parents have been stay-at-home moms, painters, carpenters, doctors, bikers, teachers, sales people, police officers, paramedics, fire fighters, and postal carriers; some had been in jail or were alcoholics/addicts; one was a pastor. But each one taught me something important that has changed my life forever. They are the parents of my students and we have to find a way to work together.

> One parent was a teacher before she had her children. As a regular volunteer in my classroom, she would talk about the educational courses she had taken and we would discuss how they related to our students and their learning. This parent was a real support for me as an educator. Many other parent volunteers have offered a lot to the class program and their own personal ideas about how children learn best.

What works best for me is to make a point of getting to know the parents of my students. With parents who are challenging and resistant to listening to what I have to say, I go out of my way to get to know them and develop a positive relationship. I want to be their friend and usually they become mine. Parents who resist this connection may have had previous negative experiences with a school. They can't see how their resistance to connect could get in the way of their child's success at school. Sometimes they have given up on their child and don't know where to turn; I try to help them believe they can finally feel hope for their child.

> A child's family was exasperated by his behavior. To our knowledge, we had done everything we could at school to help this child feel included and cared for. On a regular basis, however, he would get an upset stomach after lunch and have to go home for the afternoon. Our resource team debated about what to do. Was this an emotional response to being at school or did he have a medical issue? Unfortunately the child didn't have a regular doctor; on top of that, he had challenging learning and physical needs. Our resource team at school decided that I would take this child and his mother to the children's hospital. We needed an expert opinion. When I arrived at the hospital, I noticed that the child's mother wasn't giving the receptionist enough information about her son and his condition. The doctor needed to know that her son was autistic, and would be unable to perform certain tasks or understand what he was being asked. Someone who was not aware of the child's condition might think he was being uncooperative, because the child could present as being normal. When we shared this information with a nurse, the nurse intervened when the doctor started to examine the child and shared this pertinent information. The way the child was treated changed immediately.
>
> It so happened this young doctor was starting his own medical practice and wanted to build his clientele with special-needs children. When he found out that the child didn't have a family doctor, he asked if he could be the child's regular doctor. The young mother was delighted and agreed to the doctor's request. Upon further examinations at later appointments, the doctor found that the child suffered from a rare intestinal problem and his inability to digest his lunch properly caused the stomachaches.

You might think you know everything about a child, but parents can always enlighten you more. I will always remember an important conversation I had with a parent I had contacted because I thought her child was not playing cooperatively with another child at recess. The child was very impulsive and regularly had problems getting along with his peers. I thought this was one of those times. The parent asked me questions: Did I know that the problem with her son had started the day before when other children were being hurtful toward him? Was I aware that the problem was continuing that day and her son was trying to defend himself? I realized that I had not taken the time to ask enough questions and unfortunately assumed her son had started the problem that day.

I can count on one hand the number of parents I've met over the years who weren't interested or ready to talk about how their child could be helped, usually because they felt their child didn't need help. It is a life-long process to accept a child's challenges. Ignoring them doesn't make them go away. Experience has taught me that the sooner we get a handle on a child's strengths and needs, the sooner the child will have the supports and direction he/she needs to be successful. Young children often are more able to accept and deal with their disabilities than older students. Being young gives students more time to start to feel comfortable and knowledgeable about their challenges and begin to experience success earlier in their lives. Some students need only a few years of guided practice before they can be independent in their learning. When help is provided to children when they are young, they don't experience the same frustration and negative behaviors as an older student would; their road to success is much faster and quicker.

There are several strategies you can use to bring parents into the relationships you have with your students:

- Have daily conversations with parents as they drop off their children or pick them up after school. This helps parents feel comfortable and open to sharing how their day is going, and leads to developing a working relationship that supports their child.
- Organize classroom orientations with families at the beginning of each school year to talk about the curriculum that will be covered and how parents can support their child. Invite parents to attend evening meetings to better understand the class learning. Attend whole-school evenings where teachers and students organize Math or Writing Nights, and when students welcome their parents to celebrate their learning through portfolio evenings throughout the year.
- Consider home visits to visit students in their homes. Make regular phone calls home to inform parents of their child's learning and make sure concerns are dealt with immediately and not saved up for parent–teacher meetings months away. You can share a positive observation with the parent, something that will make them proud or happy for their child.
- Work with parents to set goals for their child's learning.
- Post classroom newsletters online and make them available to families in print.
- Encourage parents to volunteer their time in class or help from home by completing organizing tasks that will lessen the classroom preparation load. Help can also be given during school excursions into the community.

Daily Conversations

Welcome parents daily when they are dropping their child off or picking them up after school. Greet them with a smile and take time to have conversations so you can hear about their day, find out about interests and concerns. I welcome these conversations each day because parents let me know if their child had a great morning or whether they need more patience from me today. It gives me useful information about the child for the rest of the school day.

I have had the good fortune to meet numerous grandparents trying to parent their grandchildren so they will have better, productive lives. They always taught me a lot about being humble, about the power of love, and to never give up.

I met a loving grandmother who was parenting her grandson. During some of our conversations, she shared her former struggles as a parent with addictions. She wanted a better life for her grandson so he wouldn't suffer the same losses that her children suffered during their childhood. While her children still struggled with their own battles, she wanted to make a difference in her grandson's life by being a positive parent for him so he could become a successful adult.

> Another grandparent I worked with had many health issues herself but still always had her door open for her grandchildren. She knew what they needed and wanted to give it to them. Even when her grandchildren had children of their own, they were welcome to come and live with her. She wanted to support them.

My conversations with parents change and evolve as we slowly establish a relationship dialogue. Parents take home ideas from these conversations and start to reflect and think further about some issues. They may start to take a closer look at their child and/or themselves; do they need to make some changes in parenting their child? They may have some *aha!* moments when old knowledge connects with new ideas. As a teacher, I can be part of that learning curve on which we are all learning together.

I have found that being a parent of a special-needs child gives me credibility with other parents with special-needs children. I know and they know that there is nobody better to talk to about your special-needs child than another parent who has been there. You aren't judged and you don't have to explain how you feel. I feel that, as a teacher, I get to say a lot more to these parents than I would otherwise. But I'm careful to start out slowly because I don't want to scare them away. Developing connections is a gentle dance of taking one step at a time; the tempo quickens and the steps can get trickier only when you have built a sense of trust between you and your partner. You want to let parents know that there is a light at the end of the tunnel. There are lots of positives and supports in the community to help you and your family.

> I had many conversations with a parent whose child had violent and out-of-control behavior at home and at school. The parent would usually come with tears in her eyes because she felt there was no hope for her child. I met frequently with her and Childrens' disAbility Services support staff, and eventually she was allowed a respite worker that would take her son out so she could get a break at home. Her son also participated in additional programs that over time helped him to be less volatile with changes in his daily routine and helped him retain new information. As a team, we never gave up and soon she saw hope for her child.

Daily conversations help to open the doors to understanding of different points of view. I remember having a conversation with one student's parents and their struggle with how classroom goals fit into their personal religious beliefs. Their child could not celebrate some of the school seasonal activities, such as Halloween and Christmas. By being open to their beliefs and adjusting their child's program, I let our discussions lead to a situation in which they felt their beliefs were respected even though I may not have agreed with them. I have found that when parents feel you are listening to their thoughts and concerns, they are more able to accept a situation in which their concerns don't always change the course of your actions in class. In the end you will still be able to work together as a team.

> I remember going for coffee with a parent who had emigrated from another continent. Her social customs were very different from what was acceptable in parenting children in Canada. In her country, parents often had unrealistic expectations of their children; children would be disciplined through corporal punishment. As a single parent to three elementary students, she had a heavy load to carry on her own. She was harder on her daughter than on her two sons, and expected more of her. I hoped our honest conversations gave her support to change some of her parenting practices. I know I learned a lot about her culture and the horrors of living through a civil war. Years after she moved to another country, she phoned me one Christmas to say she was thinking of me and to give me updates about her wonderful children. Our renewed conversation was a special Christmas gift.

By partnering with the parents of your students, you can encourage them to talk about concerns they have for their children and help them develop a plan to meet these issues. This connection might help parents gather the courage to meet with other professionals to discuss their child's needs in more detail to gain even more support.

Organizing Classroom Orientations

Each year, I invite families to class for a beginning-of-the-year orientation and to hear about their children's learning for the year. Before Christmas and Easter breaks, parents are invited back to hear how their children's learning is progressing and if extra help or supports are needed. Most schools have students attend with their parents so they can display and describe the work they have completed so far. The whole community of learners should be welcomed with their parents and families to the school meeting. There are positives to share about all children and all children love to hear these positives from their teachers and parents.

I recommend that you avoid asking for meetings with only the parents of children who need extra support. It can be awkward if all parents attending have children who are either in trouble or need extra help. Organize separate earlier meetings to talk in detail about students with challenges; these meetings can be organized throughout the year as the need arises so the child's team takes care of learning and behavior issues right away. Students don't attend these meetings with their families unless there is a specific plan to share with the child and his/her input is needed.

Through the years I have prepared video presentations for parents so they can see the learning their children are involved with in the classroom. Parents are invited to school in the evening to watch the videos and talk about the learning with other parents. There is nothing like watching your children busy at learning. Teaching Kindergarten, I loved to tape the students' learning through play. I would write a script and read it as the parents watched the tape. It showed the learning as being very hands-on and made it easy for parents to see how their children were growing. During those meetings, I would make suggestions to parents about how they could add to their child's learning at home. In this way, we were supporting each other and working together.

I was invited to attend a parent meeting for one of my own children. The invite letter stated that you should only attend if your child has behavior or learning issues. In attending that school meeting I felt like a marked person, along with every other parent there that evening.

When students organize portfolio evenings to share their work with their parents, children lead their own interviews and share all they know about their specially prepared work. I get students involved in planning the whole portfolio evening. This is another opportunity for students to take responsibility for their learning. Their parents become part of the process too, sending supplies, etc., to help with the preparation and organization. This makes the evening a community event.

Sometimes potluck barbecues would be included in our presentations. Families would come after work, have a bite to eat, and be involved in some classroom learning. I still have a colored glass bowl from one of our barbecues. No matter how I tried to return it to its rightful owner, nobody declared it as their own. When I use this bowl, great memories return and remind me of past student–family friendships and all the food, ideas, and stories shared with our class.

> At one school we had a Roots of Empathy program, in which a parent with a newborn child is paired with a classroom they visit monthly. Students watch the baby grow and learn how to connect with the baby by reading about how children develop in the first year and what they could do to encourage this growth. A classroom bulletin board is devoted to pictures of the child at different stages and students holding and encouraging the baby to try playing with new toys. The program teaches children how to show empathy, kindness, and respect for others.

Home Visits and Phone Calls

Home visits are beneficial to building a positive relationship between the family and school. Many parents feel more comfortable in their own surroundings and approach the meeting relaxed and more willing to share. They are proud of their home and feel honored that you have taken the time to come. They usually welcome you with a beverage and a comfortable spot to sit and talk.

When I was a Kindergarten teacher, my school division expected us to start the school year by visiting our students and their families at home. I always looked forward to these visits because parents loved showing me what their children were able to do. Students loved getting extra attention, being read to, and talking about the books they enjoyed. This initial connection with my students' families helped me find parents willing to volunteer to help in class and on school outings, or to share a special talent with the class. It was a very positive start to the school year.

As a student services teacher, I made a point of visiting a student at home with his classroom teacher. We found that the home setting helped us to share more about the student's progress. Meeting in the family home helped the parents relax and talk more openly about their child's needs. The teacher and I realized that, while this student was able to move around in a wheelchair at school, his home was not fitted with any ramps. He could not get into and out of his home on his own. The family agreed to work with the child's occupational therapist and physiotherapist to apply for funding to have ramps installed at home.

> I once visited a home when parents were unable to come to the portfolio evening at school. Their child was disappointed she couldn't share her work with her parents. In past years, she had had frustrating environmental pressures, but that year in Grade 6 she was connecting, making friends, and having success in learning. The child's face beamed with pride as she shared her work with her excited, happy parents. This home visit showed her parents that she had become successful at school.

When you have to talk to parents about a concern, always ask them first how they can help you solve the issue with their child. Parents know their children best and will have many useful strategies to help you out. This idea was shared with me by a colleague who was a master teacher and deeply respected by his students and parents.

It's a good idea to phone all your students' parents in the first month of school to talk about the positive growth you are seeing in their children. This lets them know that you care about their children and want them to be successful. Never leave having conversations about a student struggling with a problem until formal parent–teacher meetings; parents want to know immediately. This way you can work on a solution right away so the child can get back to being a successful learner.

You will find that parents will be more supportive of your ideas if you take time to share the positives as well as the negatives with them. Try to put yourself in the parents' shoes to understand how they feel: it's not easy parenting a challenging child. If you let them know they have teacher and school support, it will go a long way toward helping them make the best decisions for their child.

> I once met a combative, volatile child who was only in Grade 2. He would regularly have meltdowns, flee the class, and run out into the playground. School was a horror for him, but his mother shut herself off from the school. I made a point of regularly phoning her to point out the positives I observed in her son during the day. Slowly she started to open up to me about her challenges as a parent. She became comfortable enough to invite me to accompany her and her son to a doctor's appointment. I was able to describe to the doctor the learning challenges the child experienced daily. The doctor began to see the child's learning and social difficulties in a different light and was able to look past the fact that the mother had cancelled appointments, causing her son to miss most of his important booster shots. The mother gave me written permission to contact the child's doctor with continued concerns, and the student was later referred to psychiatry for further assessments and appointments to support his development. With this support, the child started to make some positive gains in his learning and his explosive outbursts decreased. This mother needed a friend, somebody she could trust.

Setting Goals Together

See pages 27–31 for parent and student surveys.

It's important to share with parents goals for student learning, rules for behavior, and learning expectations for the coming school year. A colleague came up with a list of procedures and rules that empowered students to work both independently and cooperatively with peers in class, a plan to stay focused and be positive learners. In August he made a database for his upcoming students and sent letters to their home to welcome them to his Grade 7 classroom. He attached a survey for students and their parents that asked about their interests. They were encouraged to include questions about his program and share any concerns. This teacher was setting the stage for connecting and building a solid relationship with his students and their families.

This educator remembered a time when he was 16 and spent the evening frustrated and upset because he didn't know how to complete an assignment that was due the next day. His parents were unable to help him because they didn't understand either. Now as a teacher, he encourages parents and students to contact him whenever they have questions or concerns. Parents are given his phone number and e-mail address so no child would waste a night at home worrying how to finish an assignment.

When procedures are put into place, they promote responsibility and teamwork. Having clear expectations eliminates a lot of unnecessary negative behaviors and ensures that students have the optimum learning environment. Parents and teachers want to set reasonable expectations for their child's learning at the beginning of the year and update these expectations as the child grows and develops throughout the year. Goals can be as simple as setting a time for a student to leave from home in the morning so he/she can arrive at school on time. For students who have a hard time transitioning from home to school, a morning and afternoon check-in with an adult can help them start their day and afternoon ready for learning. Use the Student Check-in instructions on page 76.

The Five-Point Scale (Buron & Curtis, 2003) helps a child to get to know his/her social and emotional strengths and needs. Time needs to be taken to walk through this scale with the child to review what the numbers from 1 to 5 mean:

1: the child is calm and happy.
2: the child is calm but needing to move.
3: the child is starting to get unsettled and feeling not happy.
4: the child needs to get up and leave; is feeling like he/she is getting out of control.
5: the child is out of control, unable to stop him/herself and needs to leave.

This scale can help students look at their behavior, talk about how they feel at each stage, and come up with ideas of how they can better control themselves at each stage. It helps children take responsibility for their behavior because they are involved in developing their own scale with their teacher.

For some students and their families, it takes many phone calls home, conversations at school, and attending school information evenings before you can set goals together as a team for the child. When you arrive at this point, there is trust, and it becomes an easy process to set goals for the child. You continue your phone calls home and daily conversations, and take time to meet to keep everyone updated with the student's progress.

> It is also important to communicate with the home openly about technology and online safety. The Canadian Centre for Child Protection has developed many useful programs for parents, students, and teachers for safe use of technology.

I remember making many phone calls to a mom about her twin daughters. She was dissatisfied with the programming they were receiving and the relationship issues they had with other students. Each daughter had her own strengths, and through my conversations with their mother, I learned more. Their mother worked during the day, so she appreciated phone calls after work. We were able to talk and put plans in action for the students. We set goals for the classroom programming. The students were going to work on getting along with their peers and their mom was taking them to counselling once a week. Through conversations, working with the students, and outside counselling, we were able to develop workable goals that the students could participate in developing.

In another situation, a parent had cut herself off from the school, making it very difficult to discuss her son's behavior and learning needs. After many phone calls I was invited to her home to hear how she was dealing with her son in the community. This discussion opened the doors to more communication between the school and home. Over time, we were able to set goals for her son, goals he was involved in creating and carrying out. He agreed to help with the school recycling program and would go from class to class with his instructional assistant to pick up items for recycling. Also, he loved to make videos of his dinosaur collection and tell a story; his life goal was to direct a movie. This student developed the confidence to share his talents with his class peers and began to complete more work in class. It was important to meet daily with him to review his goals and give him encouragement to carry out these goals every day. We developed a daily schedule that he could look at every morning and every afternoon to see what would happen next.

Class and School Websites

Set up your classroom website so that students and their families can access it at home. Students can have shared responsibility for keeping your classroom website updated and current. Schedules with an outlined job list can be posted directly above the classroom computer so students can check to see when they have a turn.

Families can use the class website to access information about upcoming school events, due dates for school projects, tests/exams, and daily homework. You might make a point of encouraging your parents and students to e-mail you when they have questions or need you to phone them.

It's helpful to have a monthly schedule for students and parents. They will see school outings coming up, a need to hand in permission forms ahead of time, extra materials that might need to be taken to school for a project, and having to dress for a particular outing or presentation. When my class has a lot to share we put it into the school or classroom newsletter. A newsletter can give students practice in writing about their class projects, and include interesting news about students and their hobbies.

Consider printing copies of the monthly schedule and newsletters for families that don't have computers or access to the Internet. Students can take these home as soon as they are printed.

Parent Volunteers

I have always enjoyed welcoming parents to my classroom when they volunteer their help. Parents can help when we go on outdoor education outings together; we can each look after smaller groups of students and be available to give the children more attention and support. Parents who are unable to help in the classroom can prepare parts of lesson activities at home; they can design activities on their computer, and aid in the organizing of these materials. Most of my students' parents are able to help bake or cook for special occasions and many have come to class to show the students how to prepare a special ethnic dish and share their recipes. I have had both mothers and fathers volunteering in my classroom.

> When Kindergarten students were studying community helpers in social studies, we were able to invite people from our neighborhood flower shop, bakery, gas station, library, food store, and law office to come into class to talk with students about their jobs. We prepared for each visitor by discussing what we thought his/her job entailed, looked for books about his/her career in our school library, and wrote down ideas that we brainstormed together after our discussion and readings. We had a great time welcoming our career visitors to class and students took turns asking questions. After each visit we would write a class story about everything we learned from our visitor and draw pictures to highlight each point. These books were kept in our class library for everyone to enjoy; students could take the books home to share with their families.

Parent volunteers are great ambassadors for our classroom and school community, positively supporting our programs and learning in the community. They are genuinely welcomed to my classroom and our school, and receive special training at the beginning of the year regarding confidentiality and making sure information regarding all students stays within the school. If they have any concerns regarding students, they are encouraged to share with me or the school administration. As the classroom teacher, you have the final say as to how your volunteers will support class learning. Place your volunteers where they can be the most help.

I have been lucky over the years to have talented, caring, helpful parent volunteers who have added more knowledge, skills, materials, ideas, and love to my classroom program. In an early-years classroom, a grandmother came to show students how to make pasta from scratch. Students were shown how to measure flour and salt, add an egg and water, and, with lots of kneading, get the dough ready to pass through the pasta cutting machine. Students were amazed to see what they were able to make with such simple ingredients. We boiled the pasta and added some sauce and cheese for our snack that day. It was delicious!

Parents might run our school vision and hearing screening programs, lunch programs, and parent advisory committees. They can give students extra practice through the speech and language clinician's language program or the resource and classroom teachers' reading programs. During the school day, parents enjoy keeping my centres organized. I always need a lot of help in this area because our students are moving through their assignments quickly and on to the next challenge, so it helps when their work can be filed away quickly. Parents come from all walks of life with the willingness to be mentors in the classroom. Research has proven that parental involvement has a positive impact on a child's learning potential. Children learn more when their parents are involved in their education and they love their parents' presence in class.

Most school concerts and musicals are supported by parents making costumes, helping their children practice their lines at home, and getting them to school in the evening for extra practices. I worked at a school where one of the school visions was to make sure all our parents felt welcomed at school. Our school serviced an area where families lived in poverty and had previous negative experiences with the school system. We wanted all our parents to feel special

---

I remember working with an exceptional educational assistant at one school; she explained that after her students graduated from the school, she decided to get further training and become an educational assistant.

so, when we had concerts or musicals, we would have special round tables covered with tablecloths in our gymnasium for families to sit at. Our teachers and students would serve desserts and coffee for families to enjoy during the school performance. Our community really felt special and cared for.

Student Check-In

Date: _____

Student Name: _____ Time:_____ a.m. or p.m.

The Five-Point Scale

1: the child is calm and happy.
2: the child is calm but needing to move.
3: the child is starting to get unsettled and feeling not happy.
4: the child needs to get up and leave; is feeling like he/she is getting out of control.
5: the child is out of control, unable to stop him/herself and needs to leave.

Adapted from Buron and Curtis (2003) *The Incredible Five Point Scale*

1. Greet student at the door or at the front office. This is decided ahead of time so it becomes routine

2. Move to a quiet space; e.g., the library, calming room, multi-purpose room.

3. Have a conversation with the student about how he/she is feeling. Have student mark his/her Five-Point Scale.

4. If student is 3 or above, brainstorm with student as to how he/she can move to 2 or 1.

5. If student needs activity to calm down, check if you can use equipment in resource room, gym.

6. Review how student is feeling now and where he/she is on the Five-Point Scale

This meeting helps prepare the student for walking into the classroom and focusing on their work. An adult may need to walk with the student to class and stay with the student a few minutes to help the transition to class.

6

The Teaching Community

The School Team

As I work hard to develop my classroom team of students and parents, I have school administration, student services, educational assistants, and teaching colleagues as the core of my School Team. We need to include these people when we look at supporting our students, as each has a special role in ensuring student success. Make sure to bring them onto your student/parent/teacher team.

School Administration

I have worked under the tutelage of many fine administrators whose leadership was awe-inspiring and made me want to be a better educator. One principal would always bring new ideas to staff meetings and was excited and eager to hear staff thoughts. He breathed love for teaching and learning and had faith in all of us. His passion for new strategies and refining our school goals was always present. He was a perfect example of how to treat students respectfully. From the time he was a classroom teacher, he made sure he didn't embarrass or make his students feel uncomfortable, and he carried this through to being an administrator. He thought it was important to let children know when they made a mistake and to be there to encourage them to be successful again.

This work ethic is what I daily try to bring to my class. I want it mirrored in my discussion with my administrator. Over the years I have taken time to invite my administrator to my classroom. When I taught Kindergarten, I asked my principal to listen to my students sing their favorite songs. When he walked into my Kindergarten class while students were playing in their centres, he wasn't sure that they were engaged in learning, but during his visit he was thrilled to see all the work they had put into learning many songs. My classrooms, over the years, have invited our principal to join special cultural lunches, writing sharing circles, reading groups, and outdoor education trips. An administrator will get to know children better by spending an afternoon or morning with them, having conversations, and observing how each student behaves and thinks.

It's important to let your principal know when issues arise with your students so he/she can be prepared at the office and deal with it as it comes their way. Principals appreciate being kept on top of the latest happenings with students so, when parents or the community phone to talk about a situation, they will have had time to think about the incident and come up with solutions and strategies. For example, if you have a particular child who has stopped listening to you, ask your administrator to be part of the solution so the child starts to follow your lead again. I had a student who refused to complete some work; he thought that, when the school bus arrived, he would be going home and not have to complete his work. I arranged with his mother and the principal that I would keep him after

---

School administration has access to many resources, so it's important for them to know what your plans are with your students and what resources you will need to accomplish them. There won't always be funding for new equipment, but there could be connections to resource people for collaboration and new divisional initiatives.

As an administrator, I like to arrange times to meet and talk with teachers about their teaching goals and how students are working in their classrooms. I want to find out what is important to them in teaching, how they go about achieving it, and what experiences they bring to their present teaching. As a teacher, I enjoyed having my administrator observe my class and conference later on with his/her findings.

school that day. The student would complete his work and then I would drive him home. This quickly got the student to start completing his work every day.

I think it's important for students and their families to see their teacher and administrator talking and sharing important information. Knowing the staff and office work collaboratively together helps develop further confidence in the school. We are all partners in the children's learning. I like to have my administrator attend some of my student–parent meetings as a support and to learn more about the student's needs and talents. Sometimes my principal's presence will give more importance to the meeting. If I want the meeting to be more low-key, I wouldn't ask him/her to attend. When there are challenging behaviors and learning issues, my administrator would need to attend all meetings to play an integral part in supporting this student in the school.

Often in these meetings I fulfill the role of the helpful, understanding person, while my principal is the face of the school and divisional policy. It's a good idea to work out this scenario first, so that you can coordinate your information and, in the end, there is still one person who is the friend of the parent and child, someone the parent will talk to and accept suggestions and directions from. Sometimes parents know they need to change but need time to sort through it and get themselves ready. As the classroom teacher, I can work slowly with them and continue to encourage them. The principal will stand for a bottom line that parents will have to meet.

> A student brought some marijuana to school. When his friends shared this information with the teacher, we needed to do a locker check and get the police involved. This issue had to be dealt with immediately, because the student needed to understand appropriate consequences for his actions. His parents were contacted and the child was dealt with by administration, who carried out the divisional policy of requiring students to attend drug counselling and to spend some time out of school. We had the student spend this time in the office, isolated from other students, so we could keep him out of the community during the day. If he spent the suspension at home on his own, there would be nobody with him to ensure he stayed home and worked on school work.

Teaching Colleagues

My classroom colleagues are my best support at school. I make sure to work at developing friendships with them because working together as a team is always fun and extremely effective. I find it helps to lighten everyone's load when we share our plans, ideas, and support together. I can help support their students when we are in the hallway, out at recess, on lunch-hour duty, coaching and monitoring intramural sports, and during student/teacher planning committees. They, in turn, support my students in all of these areas.

When you take time to develop professional relationships with your teaching colleagues, many times you are building lifelong friendships. This friendship is built on similar interests, beliefs, and goals. Whether or not you develop a close friendship, you still have the comfort of knowing a colleague next to you is there to listen or just give you a smile and a wish for a pleasant day. You and your fellow teachers are part of a larger community, the school community.

I like to be involved in recognizing other teachers for their hard work and dedication. In one school division there was a yearly request for teachers and administrators to nominate hard-working, passionate teachers for developing new teaching strategies for reading, math, and writing, or for designing a collaborative project that involved students. It is always great to get together to celebrate each other's successes. Sometimes teachers were given release time to plan collaborative units that would benefit all students. The units were shared with the whole school division to help reach the goal for the year to further develop a particular curriculum concept.

It's helpful for teachers to keep up with new research and embrace these new ideas in their teaching. Individual schools and school divisions encourage book clubs and usually provide these resources free to teachers so they support continued dialogue between professionals in the area of new reading and math assessments, writing continuums, social and emotional development in young children, etc.

Meeting with my colleagues about their current students helps me to prepare myself for working with their students next year. When meeting each spring with earlier-grade–level teachers, everyone's input is necessary. At these meetings, the students' current teachers share their student-learning and behavior information so next year's teacher can get to know their new students and be ready to support their learning in the fall. As the receiving teacher, you will want to know everything so you can arrange your classroom to continue to engage your students in learning. At these meetings you can look at which students work well together, parent requests, student requests to be with certain friends, classroom dynamics, students with special funding for learning, and behavior and community needs. As the sending teacher, you can provide the same detailed information for next year's teacher.

Student Services/Resource/Guidance

As a resource teacher, I worked in a Grade 3/4 classroom with the teacher and students to develop a guided reading program that the whole class used. We met several times a cycle to work with students in their small, leveled reading groups. This classroom needed a lot of modeling of expected classroom behaviors. A list of these behaviors was tacked on the wall and reviewed with students at the start of each class. Our students' reading and writing skills improved after this collaborative teaching approach.

The student services professional or resource/guidance teacher is the glue of school programming and the connection between students, teachers, and parents. Educators in these positions have the assessments, resources, and connections within the school division and outside agencies to be able to support every child's learning program with the team of parent, child, teacher, educational assistant, and administration. They often hear about needs of incoming students before the school does, and are the first to connect with the new family before they arrive at school. This teacher collects all the important information schools can provide to properly program and support a new student. In some school divisions, resource and guidance teachers have separate job responsibilities. A guidance teacher looks after the counselling of students with their families and/or peers, develop social/emotional skills, and help in career planning. The resource teacher looks after academic planning for students in collaboration with teachers and families. In some school divisions these two jobs are combined. When I talk

With the recent crop of books and research around balancing the academic and socio-emotional learning of students, it's important that teachers have time to review with their peers the importance of combining academic and social and emotional learning for students in their daily work.

about resource teachers in this book, I am referring to the combined position of resource and guidance counselling.

You will want to have a constant dialogue with your resource teacher so he/she knows how your students are performing and if you have any concerns about their learning. It is helpful to keep current observations and samples of student work to share when discussing learning issues; a picture and/or a writing sample can say a lot about a student's skills. Try to plan regular meeting times with your resource teacher so you can have an ongoing dialogue about your students and the opportunity to brainstorm possible measures to look further at behavior or academic issues. This person can also schedule to work with your students once or twice a cycle, giving them extra practice in their reading, math, or writing skills.

The resource person can be an additional advocate for your students and can, through their assessments and further observations, pinpoint the child's areas of need. This person meets regularly with the school, psychologist, social worker, and administration to review the whole school's student needs. Resource teachers will start the referral process when a specialist is needed for further testing and will attend meetings while you outline to parents what next steps need to be taken in order to receive further supports for one or more students. A resource person may even take the lead to chair the meeting with the parent and child.

As the classroom teacher, you want to feel that the School Team understands your concerns around your student(s) and has possible solutions that you can, with their support, carry out in the classroom. Do you need extra training to develop more understanding around a new concept? If they have recommended that your student use digital programs, do you feel competent to support your student in this? Who will train you and the child's educational assistant to use the program with your student? While you are excited to have more resources at your fingertips to support your students, you need to know that your administration, resource personnel, and other support personnel are there to support you in the process.

Classroom Support

Educational assistants are a vital member of the child's support team. Always take time to let your educational assistants know you appreciate their strengths and the important job they do with students. Work on building a trusting relationship so they will welcome trying new ideas and suggestions and be willing to learn how to do this; they need to be able to count on our support. We are fortunate to have educational assistants as part of our support team in every school. They go out of their way to connect with students and staff and make sure students are supported.

Always welcome your educational assistants with a smile and collaborate with them to determine what needs to be accomplished for certain students. It's a good use of resources if they engage through the lesson to make sure students are understanding the concepts and then work with students at their desk or in a quieter area of the class. An educational assistant's time is valuable, so make sure they are working with students.

It's the responsibility of the classroom teacher to develop student programs, work with educational assistants to implement them, and collaborate with a resource specialist to review the student's progress. Educational assistants are masters at positively working with students so children want to complete their

As a teacher I needed to find out how to use new social/emotional programs on a student tablet. Our school speech and language consultant, along with our resource teacher, spent time with our instructional assistant, the student, and myself to make sure we knew how to use the program.

Educational assistants can use a communication book to collect information and pass it on to the next person working with a student.

work and get ahead. It's important that educational assistants attend meetings for students they are working closely with, as they have insight and knowledge about strategies the student is using to approach and complete school assignments.

Try leaving a communication book for educational assistants to write in. They can note how much work the student has completed, how they responded, and other observations. This is helpful for everyone who will be working with the student, because they will know what the student has completed and what to do next.

> After completing a student reading assessment and developing a reading program for a particular student, I worked with the educational assistant to use an online spelling program to support the student's writing and reading program. The educational assistant became very excited with her new skills and would practice in the evening to be more comfortable using the program. The daily progress of the student in this spelling program encouraged her to share this success with other educational assistants. She ended up showing them the positive aspects of the program and they began using the spelling program with other students. This educational assistant became a motivated advocate for Spelling City (spellingcity.com).

The Community Team

Social workers, psychologists, speech and language clinicians, occupational therapists, physiotherapists, and board office specialists make our community team as broad and as deep as our students require. As a classroom teacher, resource specialist, and school administrator, I have always taken the time to regularly collaborate with these professionals because they help me do a better job and provide support to my students and their families at a level that I can't alone.

To make effective use of the supports in place, you need to take the time to observe your students, assess them, and review past assessments and educational summaries of their strengths and needs. When students come into your school, you need to review files from other schools. Most school offices phone schools to have these files sent but sometimes, for many reasons, the child's educational file might not be received. Be aware that it's important to make sure it arrives; if it doesn't, then let your office know so they can search for the file and request it.

Resource people often pair up and work together to provide students and their families with joint support. I worked with a psychologist and a speech and language pathologist to support developing social skills in a student who was autistic. The speech and language clinician provided the tablet with social-emotional programs that we could work on daily with the student. There were opportunities for the student to add pictures of her friends and activities on the tablet and then have the student play the games with a friend. The psychologist gave us further help in putting together social skills programs. It was a solid team working to support this student. Our psychologist would meet with students to assess their abilities and then meet again to see if there was improvement from using specially designed programs.

Take time to find all the resources available to support students in your community. You will be astounded at what is offered to make our students' lives easier and better. You are the first and last advocate for your students. They are counting on you to take the time to find what they need to be successful.

Social Workers

Social work provides immediate support to families struggling with student learning, emotional issues, and family discord. It supports students as they move from early years, through middle years, and into high school, and is the bridge between these different levels. I have worked with social workers in small student groups to help students improve their understanding of healthy relationships and how to feel better about themselves. Social workers are invaluable resources for our students and their families because they can provide the counselling and support families need.

> Social workers provide continuity for children as they move from one school to the next. A social worker worked with a particular special-needs student from the time he attended Kindergarten until he moved into a high-school co-op education program. She supported the student's mother in dealing with health issues in the family as well. We really appreciated having all this background information to support our student.

While working as an administrator and student-services specialist, I came across a student new to our school. His classroom teacher had been away the day before and he had not cooperated with his substitute teacher. As I talked with the student and his classroom teacher, I found that the student was not helping himself at all. He started to speak rudely to his teacher and to me. The student was given some time to cool down and I went to check his file. This student had just moved from the Maritimes and had been in a different school every year before this. He hadn't had a chance to make any close friends through nine years of school, and this year he was in a new school again. He had received some support from social work earlier in his education and had been back and forth between living with his mother and living with his grandmother. It seemed this child had never been able to put down any roots over the years and he was quite alone. His mother mentioned that she was thinking of leaving her husband; this would mean another move to a new school and community for her child. The student's misbehavior with his teacher was a way of signaling he was frustrated and lonely, and wanted somebody to care. Though we had little time left in the year, I arranged for the student to talk with our social worker, who contacted his family to try to arrange meetings with them. We would make sure that his next receiving school would get him connected with social work for himself and his family.

Psychologists

Psychologists are important resources for teachers, students, and families. When students are having big problems learning, when teachers and parents have collaborated closely with the student's service teacher and administration and don't know where to turn next, a quick call to a school psychologist will help. The psychologist is trained to understand all kinds of learning disorders and possible reasons for these challenges. As a classroom teacher, you may be requested to do further screening and then pass the information back to the psychologist. Psychologists are always willing to collaborate and make suggestions. I enjoy our regular school team meetings with our social worker, psychologist, and speech and language clinician, because I learn about many new ideas and resources for students.

Psychologists can take student assessments to a more detailed level than regular classroom and student-services evaluations. Their assessments can diagnose student learning disabilities so that proper programming and supports become available for students. They can consult with teachers if assessments aren't

School psychologists have limited time in their schools because their workloads are so heavy, so usually school teams make up a list at the beginning of each year as to which students will have special psychological assessments.

possible and suggest possible strategies for teachers to consider in class. If they have time they can observe students in their classroom and make further recommendations.

In parent meetings, psychologists use helpful, easy, understandable language to explain the challenge the child may be living with. We all need this information so we can continue to support the child in our classroom. These specialists give a voice to our special-needs children so we can understand what challenges they are experiencing and to make relationship-building and learning possible for every child.

Speech and Language Clinicians

Speech and language clinicians assess student language and articulation issues. They open the doors to communication for students who have language, speech, or hearing disorders. They can bring light and hope to students and their families.

> One clinician worked with a group of parents to meet daily with our Kindergarten students to help improve some articulation challenges. With constant, regular support, the students had conquered their articulation challenges by the time they reached Grade 1. This dynamic student program was made possible by the regular training and support from our speech and language clinician and devoted parent volunteers.

A speech and language clinician can supply students with augmentative and alternative communication devices. Students can also be taught to use Signing Exact English if they are hearing impaired or deaf. I was encouraged to have the Signing Exact English alphabet of whole-word symbols in the classroom, and learned a lot about choosing to live in a language-based or symbol-based world. I came to realize and better understand that the deaf community is like living in another country. There are different social mores that can clash with those of the hearing community. I worked with a family in which both parents and their child were deaf. The father felt more comfortable in the deaf community, whereas his wife felt at ease in the hearing and deaf communities; their daughter was educated in both communities.

A speech synthesizer can be implemented through computer software or hardware products for students who are nonverbal. It gives the student a voice in their class and community. The technology keeps the student's toolbox full and makes a big difference in learning. It gives these students a variety of ways to communicate with their peers and adults. A text-to-speech system converts normal language text into speech. When students use this program, they can have a whole story read to them by pressing the cursor over the words on the computer monitor. Again this tool connects a hard-of-hearing child or a child unable to read to the sounds of the printed words.

> I was working with a student who wore hearing aids. In order to direct the conversation to him and drown out background noises, we used a sound field system in the classroom. This system absorbs background noise and makes the speaker's voice clearer and closer, helping keep all students focused on the classroom lesson. A side benefit to using this tool in your classroom is that, because the system keeps your voice clear and loud all through the classroom for all students, there is less strain on your voice.

Therapists

Occupational and physiotherapists are invaluable in supporting and assessing children's mobility and fine motor issues. They are trained to observe, assess, and design daily programs for students to support their learning. They have access to assistive mobility and technology devices for students to heighten classroom learning.

Therapists can offer practical ideas for students and their parents. At one meeting our occupational therapist suggested that a parent buy pants made of softer material for her child. When we met after the summer, the parent reported that her son's new pants made a difference. His pants were no longer too tight and uncomfortable, and his general attitude had improved. Her son was a happier child with fewer negative behaviors.

I've worked in schools where Kindergarten students had weekly movement programs to work on their gross and fine motor skills. These programs were run by parents who had been trained by occupational therapists. When students have trouble focusing, they should have lots of opportunities to move in their environment. This movement helps them stay focused and learn in their classroom. I found the program was a great way to connect with my students and their families, and to talk about movement activities in the greater community. Families were encouraged to be active with their families in the evenings and on weekends.

Physiotherapy is essential for students who have mobility impairments or weaknesses. Physiotherapists can assess a student's life skills and how to adapt the student's environment so they have accessibility in their learning space at school and in the community; they will train educational assistants and the classroom teacher in carrying out the child's daily physiotherapy program. The only student in our school who used a wheelchair to be mobile worked with a physiotherapist to plan a wheelchair obstacle course at school for himself and his recess buddies. All our Grade 3, 4, 5, and 6 students became involved in the wheelchair competition, each understanding different movement challenges and having a chance to "walk in the disabled student's shoes."

> I had a student who was legally blind but still was able to function without a cane. She received support through CNIB and we both learned a lot about how to best support her at school. This student taught me about using all our senses to help improve our ability to move freely in the community. She was always positive and knew how to ask for help. I enjoyed working with her.

As a university supervisor I recently observed students in a Kindergarten class having movement breaks when they were not able to stay quiet and focused during a lesson. After a ten-minute break, they came back to class with the educational assistant or their classroom teacher and were able to settle down and focus on the lesson.

7

Working Together as a Learning Community

Individual class or whole-school projects can be a great example of how relationships increase learning and bring the community together to work on common goals. Organized around moral intelligences, such large-scale projects use a common language that is practiced schoolwide and used in the community at large.

An Aboriginal Perspective

I will always remember the smiles on the faces of students as they took their turns walking with their partners to the middle of the gym and performing a special dance or song they had learned from our two visiting artists. Walking by their classrooms that morning, I had watched students, teachers, and parents put the last touches on costumes to make sure they fit properly. A handful of parents were busy in the staffroom, unpacking frozen breads they had helped students make and freeze several weeks before. Everyone seemed to have an important job to carry out so we could all be together in our special Making Connections assembly that afternoon. The families of our Grades 3 to 6 students were in the crowd, transfixed as they watched their children perform traditional songs and dances from many cultures: Kumbaya, Mangwani M'Poolele, Siyahamba (African); Say It in Vietnamese, Handkerchief Song, Hat Dance, Dragon Dance, Stick Jumping Dance (Vietnamese); or Native Alphabet, Ninestosin, Caribou Song, Indian Lullabye (Aboriginal). The whole school and community were present to enjoy the fruits of everyone's hard work to show what our students had learned in our Social Studies programs. We ended the afternoon by enjoying delicious bannock, masa, and buncu breads together. We were a family, enjoying months of learning and sharing our knowledge about the Aboriginal, African, and Vietnamese cultures.

Our school had spent the preceding three years working on developing moral intelligences tied into our school behavior goals. The provincial education and training department had created a document that looked at Integrating Aboriginal Perspectives into our curricula, and our school division offered funds so staff could develop a plan around including the Aboriginal perspective in daily teaching. Armed with a community that understood the benefits of teaching and expecting its members to show respect, kindness, empathy, self-control, fairness, tolerance, and conscience, we embarked on a two-year plan. Our divisional Aboriginal Academic Achievement Grant, along with support from the Parent Advisory Council and Manitoba Arts Council, provided us with the funds we needed to hire skilled artists to work with staff and students to learn Aboriginal

> I remember with fondness the special assembly planned for our K–2 students a week after the Grade 3–6 assembly. Our divisional Aboriginal Community Networker brought jiggers (students and adults) with two special fiddlers. After the jiggers finished their performance, all students were invited to the middle of the gym to jig along with the dancers. It was fun to see the students bouncing up and down and trying to lift their legs up high like the dancers. It was an awesome final performance!

traditional dancing, cooking, storytelling, and writing. To support our diverse school population, we chose to study African and Vietnamese traditions along with Aboriginal cultures. Our students and their families came from more than 40 different countries around the world. We wanted to establish a culturally responsive education for our students and develop a learning environment that promoted success for all of them. We continued to work on the moral intelligence of tolerance in order to focus on celebrating diversity.

Our first order of business was to establish a Linking Home and School Committee, with the help of our Parent Advisory Council. This committee would keep staff, students, and the community updated. Staff and parents were instrumental in making resource packages for each classroom, from Kindergarten to Grade 6, organizing resource people to visit classrooms, and planning the spring Making Connections assembly. The first year of the plan would look at exploring students' cultural roots through dance, song, music, and drama. The first residency artists worked with our Grade 3 to 6 students for two weeks in October; the second residency was in April. The artists had a bit of time to work with the Kindergarten students as well. Our music and physical education specialists met with the Grade 1 and 2 students in the area of movement, dance, and song. Our Linking Home and School Committee connected our plans with the K–4 social studies curriculum; they contacted several community leaders to come in and share their life stories.

A group of interested Grade 6 students formed a group called Student Ambassadors to welcome visitors to our school, make everyone feel comfortable at our spring assemblies, and build three cultural display walls within the school. These walls represented Aboriginal, African, and Vietnamese cultures. Families sent pictures, family photos, and stories to be displayed on the cultural walls. Classrooms would take their students to view and enjoy the walls as they were finished. A world map hanging in the office collected pins representing the countries our students and their families had emigrated from.

Kindergarten students looked at cultural celebrations. Grade 1 students studied community helpers and read books that highlighted various cultures and genders. Grade 2 students had community helper books translated into Vietnamese and read by two Vietnamese Grade 6 students. Students in Grades 3 to 6 worked with artists to learn Aboriginal, Vietnamese, and African dances and songs. An Aboriginal storyteller worked with Grade 4 students. All students, with the support and help of staff and parent volunteers, made breads from the three cultures, to be frozen and later enjoyed at the April assembly.

Teachers worked on strategies to develop positive attitudes toward diversity through the social studies curriculum dealing with Community. Students would learn to be more tolerant of their peers and come to appreciate their uniqueness. Parents were informed of their children's learning and were encouraged to have conversations with their children around what they had learned. Literacy and writing opportunities were planned for all students for the week after the two assemblies, and special writing activities were designed for K–3 classes. New books were purchased by the librarian and shared with all classrooms so students could take them home to enjoy with their families or use as they wrote about the experience of learning a new dance, song, or story.

A questionnaire was designed for Grade 5 and 6 students, another for parents and staff, to see if students benefited from the interactive cultural learning. The Linking Home and School Committee reviewed and tallied the questionnaire results. The artists felt our students were cooperative and very interested in participating in their workshops, and gave special recognition and respect for our school's diversity. Parents appreciated being part of the Linking Home and School Committee. They enjoyed being helpful and spending time in their child's school. They were happy to see their children excited about learning new dances and songs and connecting this with their social studies program. Parents who were invited to share their life stories with the students said that they felt more comfortable in the school. Students who shared their life stories felt more confident with themselves and were openly proud of their heritage. Teachers were pleased with how Student Ambassadors took their responsibilities seriously and worked hard at welcoming people and creating the three cultural walls.

For the second year of our Aboriginal Academic Achievement Grant, we felt that staff was ready to further look at how to integrate the Aboriginal perspective into daily programs. Each subject area would address the perspectives and accomplishments of Aboriginal people. Teachers arranged a half-day planning meeting with their grade-level partners to look at the following topics:

- Historical Timeline: a list of events significant to the Aboriginal People of Manitoba
- Aboriginal People in Manitoba: a look at the First Nations living in our province
- Cultural and World View: including The Land, Generosity, Oral Tradition, Spirituality, Medicine Wheel, Powwows, Elders
- Education: traditional Aboriginal education

Teachers gathered the information and fit it into the Early Years (K–4) and Middle Years (5–6) learning outcomes. This information was written into our school plan. It was available to new staff and for teachers to review on a yearly basis. Our music and physical education specialists met to review how the Aboriginal perspective would fit into their programs. Teachers were able to organize cross-curricular plans involving language arts, mathematics, music, and physical education.

There were lots of exciting suggestions for future planning. Teachers wanted to have the time to plan like this with their grade-level partners the following year; they would use this time to write up a summary of their meeting. Staff also thought it would help to have a resource person come in to talk about what it would look like to add the Aboriginal Perspective to their lessons. Teachers would have lessons written up ahead of time and share with the consultant for feedback. They thought it would be important to invite more guests into classes so that students could learn more about their cultural groups, and to be able to purchase more books for the library to reflect this new class learning.

Many teachers had already gone out into the community to continue searching for more information and resources available for their class. They didn't want to wait until next year because their class was having so much fun moving forward in their learning now. At all levels, the excitement was leading to more learning:

- A class of Grade 2 students sent letters to a Grade 2 class on a northern reserve; the students developed friendships and wrote back and forth to each other all the time. All Grade 2 classes visited a museum and created an Aboriginal anthology of retellings and artwork based on 6 + 1 Traits of writing.
- Grade 3 teachers developed a special assembly with their students so they could sing "O Canada" in Cree. In class they looked at how the moral intelligences tied into the Seven Teachings.

- The Grade 4 students studied the Inuit people for their Resource Based Learning. They first went to the museum to view displays on Inuit and other Aboriginal cultures. They attended a special museum class to learn more about the Inuit.
- Teachers collaborated with the physical education teacher to organize an Aboriginal Games for the students. The music specialist introduced her students to music and songs of the Plains Indian Nations (Blackfoot, Cree, Anishinabe, Dakota, and Lakota).

The two-year plan motivated teachers to organize more curriculum resources and programming for their students. Teachers did additional teaming with their grade-level partners, sourced new books for their classrooms and school library, and built resource lists and websites to find further help in differentiating their programs for all of their students. Our school was an exciting place to be.

In this excitement I partnered with another teacher to plan a presentation for our divisional conference on Valuing the Whole Child. Our presentation, An Aboriginal Perspective Working in the Classroom, looked at how to put the Aboriginal perspective into our class reading program. We based our presentation on *The Legend of the Indian Paintbrush* by Tomie de Paola. We discussed ways to allow students a hands-on experience with the story: having a scavenger hunt at the museum; making dioramas; and using the 6 + 1 Traits of writing as tools to develop a deeper understanding of the Aboriginal culture and a measure of the children's present understanding.

Our Aboriginal Worker connected our school to a free summer sports camp for our Aboriginal students. Teachers just needed to recommend students between the ages of 7 to 12 to attend the Winnipeg Aboriginal Sport and Recreation Association Summer Kids Camps (WASAC). Our students participated in sports, cultural, and recreational activities and had a great time.

By carefully executing our two-year Aboriginal Academic Achievement Grant, we opened the minds of everyone in our community regarding the beauty of the Aboriginal culture. Students experienced the culture through their peers, families, and Elders sharing at school and in the community. We also learned more about African and Vietnamese cultures. The whole community worked on the project for two years to work at getting the Aboriginal perspective into our daily teaching. We provided all ethnic groups in our school opportunities to participate and share their cultures. Everyone benefited from these connections as everyone became closer. This project developed close friendships among school staff, parents, students, and the school community. It was a very successful and rewarding community project.

> Opikihiwawin is a group designed to give support to families who have adopted Aboriginal children. As a parent having used Opikihiwawin, I shared this resource with staff and families. Parents can go to monthly meetings to meet with other parents and support specialists; this group organizes family activities so children can become closer to their Aboriginal culture. There are special student clubs and activities throughout the year and many students become supports to the organization as they become adults.

Students and their families were invited to attend a fun-filled evening of centre-based mathematics at the end of January. The intent of Family Math Night was to participate in math standards and see them in action as we strengthened the mathematical application, problem-solving, and communication skills of our students through the power of family action.

Students and teachers carried boxes, papers, and class equipment to our school gym to set up for our Family Math Night. Each grade level had several tables to set up for their math centres, and the math curriculum from K–8 was set up around the gym. It had taken us since the fall to get ready for this family evening. Families started arriving just before 6:00 pm. The

> children pulled on the arms of their parents to hurry into the gym; they had important games and work to show them. Parents sat with their children at tables and worked through different math games together. Teachers were stationed at each of the centres to help students jump from one card to the next, place card patterns on the floor, and create designs on paper. They welcomed parents and encouraged students to help their siblings. Everyone was involved and having a great time with their family. It was an exciting community event!

Good luck in developing your own community projects and experiencing the joy of working together as a school community!

Resources

Publications

Borba, Michele (2001) *Building Moral Intelligences: The Seven Essential Virtues that Teach Kids to Do the Right Thing*. San Francisco, CA: Jossey-Bass.

Buron, Kari Dunn and Curtis, Mitzi (2013) *The Incredible Five Point Scale*, 2nd ed. Lenexa, KS: Autism Asperger Publishing Company

Denton, Paula (2013) *The Power of Our Words: Teacher Language that Helps Children Learn*, 2nd ed. Montague, MA: Center for Responsive Schools.

Diller, Debbie (2015) *Growing Independent Learners: From Literacy Standards to Stations, K–3*. Portland, ME: Stenhouse.

Early Childhood Development (2011) "Public Investments in Early Childhood Education and Care in Canada in 2010" at http://www.dpe-agje-ecd-elcc.ca/eng/ecd/ececc/page10.shtml

Gordon, Mary (2005) *Roots of Empathy: Changing the World, Child by Child*. Markham, ON: Thomas Allen.

Gossen, Diane (1992) *Restitution: Restructuring School Discipline*. Chapel Hill, NC: New View.

Gray, Carol (1991) *Writing Social Stories with Carol Gray*. Arlington, TX: Future Horizons.

Green, Ross W, and Ablon, J. Stuart (2006) *Treating Explosive Kids: The Collaborative Problem-Solving Approach*. New York, NY: The Guilford Press.

Harper, Jennifer and O'Brien, Kathryn (2015) *Classroom Routines for Real Learning*. Markham, ON: Pembroke.

Herr, Norman (2007) *The Sourcebook for Teaching Science, Grades 6–12: Strategies, Activities, and Instructional Resources*. San Francisco, CA: Jossey-Bass.

Johnston, Peter (2012) *Opening Minds*. Portland, ME: Stenhouse.

Kriete, Roxann and Davis, Carol (2014) *The Morning Meeting Book*, 3rd ed. Montague, MA: Center for Responsive Schools.

McCallum, Deborah (2015) *The Feedback-Friendly Classroom*. Markham, ON: Pembroke.

Pate, Elizabeth and Andrews, Gayle (2006) "Research summary: Parent involvement" AMLE. Retrieved August 7, 2016 from http://www.amle.org/TabId/270/ArtMID/888/ArticleID/328/Research-Summary-Parent-Involvement.aspx.

Rimm-Kaufman, Sara, et. al. (2014) "Efficacy of the responsive classroom approach: Results from a three year Longitudinal Randomized Controlled Trial" *American Educational Research Journal*, 52(3), June: 567–603.

Shore, Randy (2004) "B.C. Schools focus on educating hearts, Classrooms increasingly integrate social and emotional learning into the academic curriculum" *Vancouver Sun*, October 19.

Swartz, Larry and Lundy, Kathy (2011) *Creating Caring Classrooms*. Markham, ON: Pembroke.

Trottier, Pat (2014) Personal Interview with Grade Seven and Eight Students, February 20, 24, 27.

Wong, Harry K and Wong, Rosemary T. (2008) *The First Days of School: How to Be an Effective Teacher*. Mountain View, CA: Harry K. Wong Publications.

Websites

"abc123: reach every student" The Parent Involvement Centre at www.parentinvolvement.ca

Canadian Centre for Child Protection at https://protectchildren.ca/app/en/overview

Common Sense Media at www.commonsensemedia.org

"Early Childhood Education and Care in Canada" Child Care Canada at www.childcarecanada.org/publications/ecec-in-canada

Responsive Classroom at www.responsiveclassroom.org/

Search Institute: Discovering what kids need to succeed at www.search-institute.org

Safe Healthy Schools at www.safehealthyschools.org

Index

Aboriginal perspective, 85–89

boundaries
    class rules and, 15
    developing, 22–23
    sample, 23
    setting, 21
bowling clubs, 61

classroom
    behavior boundaries, 22–23
    management techniques, 12
    relationships in, 10–11
    responsive, 57–64
    rules, 15–17
    websites, 73
classroom community, 33–56
    developing, 33
    language of, 57–58
    group situations, 33–34
    moral intelligences, 34–42
    relationships, 10–11
classroom orientations, 69–70
classroom outings, 61–62
classroom support, 80–81
collaboration, 12, 33
community involvement, 60–61
community team, 81–84
conscience, 41–42
    class activity, 41, 42, 55
    conversations, 41
    worksheet, 42, 56
cross-curricular learning, 62–64
    described, 62
    language arts lesson, 63–64
    math lesson, 64
    science lesson, 63
crossing patrols, 20, 60–61

daily conversations, 67–69

discussions, 58
dyslexia, 58

educational assistants, 80–81
empathy, 37–38
    class activity, 37, 47
    worksheet, 37, 48

fairness, 38
    class activity, 38–39, 49
    worksheet, 39, 50
Festival de Voyageur, 34
Five-Point Scale, 72, 76

goal-setting, 71–73
group work, 33–34
guidance teachers, 79–80

home visits / phone calls, 70–71

interactive learning, 62

kindness, 35
    class activity, 35–36, 43
    worksheet, 36, 44

language of community, 57–58

moral intelligences
    conscience, 41–42
    described, 34–35
    empathy, 37–38
    fairness, 38–39
    kindness, 35–36
    respect, 36–37
    responsive classroom, 11
    self-control, 39–40
    social stories and, 58
    strategies, 34
    tolerance, 40–41

morning meeting, 18, 22, 59–60
   alphabetical order, 60
   components, 60

orientation, 69–70

Parent Invitation, 19, 27
Parent Survey, 19, 28
parental relationships, 65–76
   classroom orientations, 69–70
   daily conversations, 67–69
   described, 65–67
   home visits and phone calls, 70–71
   involving parents, 11–12
   parent volunteers, 73–75
   setting goals together, 71–73
   strategies, 67
   understanding children, 66
   websites, 73
Parents Supporting Parents, 33
physiotherapy, 84
portfolio evenings, 70
positive comments, 57–58
potluck barbecues, 70
PowerPoint, 59
principal, 77–78
provincial curricula, 62
psychologists, 82–83

questionnaires, 19, 30, 31

relationships
   caring and positive, 21–22
   in the classroom, 10–11, 33–56
   with parents, 11–12, 65–76
   with students, 9–10, 13–31
resource teachers, 79–80
respect, 16, 25, 36
   class activity, 36–37, 45
   worksheet, 37, 46
responsive classroom, 57–64
   class outings, 61–62
   community involvement, 60–61
   cross-curricular learning, 62–64
   described, 57
   language of community, 57–58
   morning meeting, 59–60
   sample lessons, 63–64
   social stories, 58–59
   strategies, 57–62
Roots of Empathy, 70

routines
   benefits, 18
   purpose of, 13–14
   types of, 18
   welcome to classroom, 17–19,
rules
   consequences of breaking, 17
   knowing, 21,
   setting, 15–17

safety, 25
schedules, 73
school administration, 77–78
school team, 77–81
self-confidence, 23–24
self-control, 39–40
   class activity, 39, 40, 51
   worksheet, 40, 52
self-regulation, 24–25
Seven Trees story, 9–10
Signing Exact English alphabet, 83
social stories, 24, 58–59
   described, 58–59
   sample, 59
social workers, 82
special needs children, 68
speech and language clinicians, 83–84
Student Check-In, 72, 76
Student Graphic Organizer, 29
Student Questionnaire, 30, 31
student relationships, 13–31
   boundaries, 22–23
   described, 9–10
   establishing enduring relationships, 25–26
   getting to know students, 19–21
   opening doors for students, 21–22
   routines, 13–14
   self-confidence, 23–24
   self-regulation, 24–25
   welcoming to classroom, 14–19
student services, 79–80
survey, 19, 28

teaching colleagues, 78–79
teaching community, 77–84
   building, 12
   classroom support, 80–81
   community team, 81–84
   psychologists, 82–83
   school administration, 77–78
   school team, 77–81

    social workers, 82
    speech and language clinicians, 83–84
    student services/resource/guidance, 79–80
    teaching colleagues, 78–79
    therapists, 84
therapists, 84
tolerance, 25, 40
    class activity, 40, 41, 53
    worksheet, 41, 54
transitions, 24

video presentations, 69
volunteers, 73–75

websites, 73
welcome to classroom, 14–19
    class rules, 15–17
    classroom set-up, 15
    routines, 17–18
    tips, 14
working together, 85–89